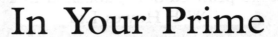

In Your Prime

Older, Wiser, Happier

India Knight

W F HOWES LTD

This large print edition published in 2015 by
W. F. Howes Ltd

Unit 4, Rearsby Business Park, Gaddesby Lane,
Rearsby, Leicester LE7 4YH

1 3 5 7 9 10 8 6 4 2

First published in the United Kingdom in 2014
by Penguin Group

A CIP catalogue record for this book is available
from the British Library

ISBN 978 1 51000 339 2

Typeset by Palimpsest Book Production Limited,
Falkirk, Stirlingshire

Printed and bound in Great Britain
by TJ International Ltd, Padstow, Cornwall

MIX
Paper from
responsible sources
FSC   FSC® C013056
www.fsc.org

For Georgia Garrett

The age thing is all up to you. It's like happiness is up to you. You just have to understand what it is before you get it.

Elaine Stritch

CONTENTS

INTRODUCTION

I'm forty-eight. That's two years away from fifty, arithmetic fans. I don't feel old. Do you feel old? I don't feel *young*, either, but I don't mind about that at all, because I'd rather be the person I am now than the person I was at twenty-five, so anxious and unsure about so many things, so tentative. I prefer forty-eight, and how. Plus I'm kinder, wiser, more patient, less judgemental. These are all improvements. Still, it's weird. I sometimes feel like a small child gazing up at a mighty statue called *The Fifty-Year-Old* with a complicated mixture of bafflement ('Eh?'), derision ('What, me? Ha, I don't think so, matey') and awe ('Bloody hell'). Fifty: the full half-century. It's absolutely absurd, and also absolutely the verifiable reality, and one of the things that annoys me about it is that I am *this* far away from saying that I am nearly 'fifty years young', a phrase that has traditionally made me want to tear off my ears and throw them on the ground in disgust. I make sounds when I sit down, too. I go 'Ooof' in a really satisfied way. I like getting into bed so much that I actually groan with pleasure – 'Wooooargh.'

Presumably you picked this book up because you're of a similar vintage (it's written for women aged from about forty to about sixty-five, roughly, but it's elastic, I hope. If you're eighty-two – welcome). Is it weird for you, this ageing malarkey? I feel exactly like I always felt, except better, in so many respects: more confident, more self-assured, more unwilling to take any crap. I mind more about the things that are important to me, and I've stopped minding about the things that aren't. Boof! They are gone.

I don't mind any more what people think about me: nobody can like everybody all the time. I don't worry about what to think, or rather about what I *should* think. I don't feel that I have to pretend to be interested in stuff that I really don't care for – like jazz or economics – in order to feel sophisticated. I'm at ease with myself, with my family, with my children. I feel liberated from all of the piddly, annoying anxieties and stresses that clogged up bits of my twenties and thirties. I genuinely feel like this is a brilliant time. Like I'm in my Prime.

The window of Prime is finite, is the thing. It's not very big. Prime comes before a fall, you might say. On the other side of Prime lies possible decrepitude – first our parents' and then our own, with all of its un-jolly adjuncts – all of the stuff we don't ever want to discuss. I mean, I don't even discuss the menopause with my friends. We sit around going, 'How do you tell? I haven't had a period in three months. Does that mean I'm *in it*?' And then we all shake our heads, saying, 'Dunno,' and feeling genuinely baffled, and we move on. The menopause is truly the last taboo, and that seems utterly nuts, given it's coming to all of us, and soon.

I wanted to write this book to help us all to maximize the Prime and to make sense of it, and then, once that was done, to lift the curtain on the un-jollities, because knowledge is power. So this is a book designed to function as a sort of manual: it's got advice about bras and Botox and advice about ailing parents, care homes and dementia. It tells you what make-up to buy and how to be a better step-parent. It has pointers for middle-aged sex and dating (I forgot 'think twice about getting on top', but I'm putting it in, as it were, here: seriously – if you're wondering why not, put a mirror on the floor and straddle it. Now look down. Yep. That's the view). And yes, of course the menopause is in here too, along with thoughts about – among other things – fashion, partying, what to do about annoying friends you've grown out of, and the traumatizing question of vaginal atrophy.

Also, are you banned from Topshop? Should you be wearing more navy blue? What are you supposed to do – where are you supposed to shop – if you want to look cool, not mumsy, even though mumsy is what you are? What about mutton? Is leopard print 'the new neutral', like magazines tell you, or are you now late-period Bet Lynch? What's going on with your teeth, by the way? Do your glasses make you feel clever, or just old – should you consider eye surgery? Does your dad have dementia? Is it bad to want to wear Big Pants all the time instead of anal floss? Two of your friends are dying – how can that be happening? Does your step-daughter hate you? Your feet hurt. WTF? That permanent soreness in your elbow – you should probably go and see a doctor about it, eh? Have you considered lying about your age? Oof, ugly bras with big thick straps are so comfy, aren't they? Macular degeneration – what's that when it's at home?

All of this stuff is made doubly, triply confusing by the fact that, traditionally, at forty-five you would almost certainly have been a grandmother. Today, you may be the mother of a toddler. You may even be both a grandmother *and* have a young child of your own. What does this make you? What's it called, and how do you manoeuvre through it?

The book you're holding contains all of the 'wisdom' I've accrued: everything useful I could possibly think of about navigating the passage to nan-dom and, crucially, navigating it joyfully. Because while even I'm not Pollyannaish enough to suggest that nothing gets worse, it's also true that an awful lot of things get dramatically better. We're in our Prime. Up and at 'em!

NB: For ease, and so that my sentences don't

get insanely long and clunky, I am assuming that the reader of this book is a woman, and I'm sticking to that assumption throughout the book. You may, of course, be of either gender, and where I say 'stepmother' I also mean stepfather, uncle, auntie, long-term live-in partner of the dad or mum, mother figure of no fixed abode, and everything in between. Equally, when I say 'husband', I also mean wife, boyfriend, girlfriend, cohabitee, partner, etc. We're a broad church, in these pages, but if I were to repeatedly start listing all possible members of the flock, this book would be 1,000 pages long.

CHAPTER 1

BEAUTY AND MAINTENANCE

Or navigating the passage from nymph to nana

I t used to be so simple, and also so awful. If you were fifty in 1955, you were a fifty-year-old matron, and there was very little deviating from this. You might, perhaps, have lived an eccentric or unorthodox existence, but you were still broadly a matron. You knew what to wear. You knew how to behave, how to speak, how to occupy yourself. The option in all of those instances was 'like a fifty-year-old matron'. They had a role, those women: matriarch or spinster. And they got it, and got on with it. They knew what they were, and how to play their part perfectly. And then feminism came along – thank God – and changed attitudes – thank God – but along with those changes came great confusion.

Take Madonna at fifty-five, five years older than my hypothetical 1950s matron above. I'm of the generation that nearly died of joy when Madonna first emerged in the early eighties, looking like a proper badass, and it follows that I have loved Madonna ever since. But, what now? Am

I supposed to want to look like her? Act like her? Be like her? Well, no, because I'm not a teenager looking for pop stars to be role models (in as much as I look to anyone, I look to Baroness Trumpington, personally). But where does Madonna fit into all of this, with her palpable and demonstrable desire for ongoing hotness and relevance? And, you know, good for her – I bet she doesn't dream about recliner chairs or sack-like clothing while she's doing her three hours in the gym, and she looks (mostly) great, and only weird sometimes, which could be true, in a different sense, of any of us.

On the other hand, I am quite annoyed with the way in which Madonna has decided to age. I feel let down by it. I wish she'd come with me and have the occasional dirty little recliner fantasy, too. She could do a book, like *SEX* except clothed, maybe called *NAN*. I'm not being facetious – I really wish she would. I wish just one woman in the public eye would relax about middle age, and I wish it were her.

CHARTING A COURSE

Now, let's take a little trip. On this island over here, you have a lovely, lush, verdant land, all fecund vegetation and swoony, head-turning blooms. And on this island over *here* you have a wintry wood. The trees are black and bare. The desiccated leaves are lying on dry ground. Nothing is green. If you look up, you can still see the sky. Unfortunately, it's raining.

Between the two islands is a narrow strait with a gentle current pulling towards the wood, and a little boat is bobbing about in the water. You're in the little boat, rowing. The question is, how hard do you row? Do you grit your teeth and head straight for the wood on the basis that, since it's going to be where the boat ends up, you may as well not waste any time? Or do you take a more leisurely approach? Do you drift and dawdle? Do you jump out and float about on your back for a bit, thinking the wintry wood can wait? Or do you straightforwardly refuse to row forward, towards the wood? Do you grab both oars and furiously row back, against the current?

Those are your choices, when it comes to ageing and looks, and we're going to take them one at a time. Before you get into the boat, though, you have to ask yourself one fundamental question. Imagine for a moment that you are not the passenger but some sort of boat-keeper. It's your boat. What you look like, or how old you are, doesn't matter – in fact, you're a man. You're a boat-man. And you have just the one boat, and this boat, this only boat of yours, is crucially important to you. It's not a new boat, by any means. Do you patch it up? Do you give it the odd coat of varnish? Do you spend days, weeks, months, fixing the boat, lovingly scraping off the

9

barnacles, so it's kept as good as new? What's important to you – that the boat works, that it functions as a boat, that it's serviceable? Or do you really cherish that boat, and hate the idea of it looking tatty, and spend a sizeable part of your time ensuring that it stays spick and span? Or maybe you think, 'It's a knackered old boat. Not much point doing anything to it, because the boat and I both know that sooner or later the boat will be buggered. As long as it stays afloat until then, I'm happy.'

Complicated business, vanity. The reason for that is the thin and under-reported line – and it's one that gets thinner with every passing year – between vanity and self-esteem. We're not talking here about a gorgeous 23-year-old who spends every spare second staring into a mirror and posting selfies to Instagram. We're talking about you and me. Forget for a moment the notion of having some sort of 'duty' to society or to your partner or to whoever to keep looking as presentable as possible for as long as possible (I'm not saying that duty – or that sense of duty – isn't real, or is insignificant, and I'll get to it in a second). What about you, though? Do you have a duty *to yourself*? Does how you look affect how you feel, what you feel capable of, how strong you feel you are?

To me, the answer to that one is an unavoidable yes. If I look like crap, I feel mildly incapacitated – like myself, but functioning at 80 per cent. Some days 80 per cent is enough, and some days it isn't. You know how, if you wander into an incredibly posh shop out of curiosity but are for some reason wearing a onesie and Uggs, the shop assistants follow you around as though you were about to nick something? It's that feeling. I spend a vast proportion of my time in onesies and Uggs, because I work from home, and I am devoted to both items. But I wouldn't go out to dinner in them. I mean, I *have* gone out to dinner in them (once) and – well, I didn't feel at the absolute top of my game, let's say.

Comfort is not always all that matters, either. I recently discovered *the* most comfortable range of clothes. They're by a Swedish woman called Gudrun Sjödén.[1] Ms Sjödén is larger, of a certain age, and likes print and colour – one of those older women who's all layers and scarves and very short hair. I was walking past her London shop and went inside because I had ten minutes to kill before meeting a friend. Well. I came out with three carrier bags of loose cotton dresses, loose cotton trousers and loose cotton tops with things like charming drawings of leaves on them. The next day my partner and I went to the seaside for the weekend, with the children. These trips are never an occasion for high glamour, but still. I came downstairs in my sturdy, shapeless dress (so comfy), shapeless trousers (mmm, the joys of

[1] gudrunsjoden.com

breathing *right* out) and a pair of Birkenstocks which for reasons of practicality – it was freezing – I had decided to accessorize with jaunty blue cashmere socks.[2] I had briefly worried, while I was getting dressed, about whether I'd gone a bit 'middle-aged art teacher'[3] and whether I should be accessorizing further with 'fun' chunky bangles or 'funky' earrings, but – no, I thought. I can style it out.

'It's more haute-hippie,' I said to myself. It's fine.

'I like your costume, Mummy,' my ten-year-old daughter said approvingly.

'Ah,' said my partner in a stupid sing-song voice. 'Vee haf come from Copenhagen, ya? Vhere ve make pottery and live alone vith our cats.'

This made me incensed, but I also laughed a lot, because it was a bit true (the clothes are great, I have subsequently worked out, but perhaps not all at once).

You may be reading this and thinking, 'Sod it, I'll go out to dinner in whatever I like,' and that's fine. I'm not passing judgement when I suggest you don't – I'm merely showing concern for your feelings of self-worth during said dinner. If they're identical to those you'd feel in a frock and heels,

[2] Can I just say, I was doing perfectly pedicured Fashion Birkenstock, this being summer 2014, rather than gnarly-toed German Artist Birkenstock. For what it's worth (not much, it turned out).

[3] See WHACKY, page 55.

or whatever your version of dressing up consists of, then congratulations: you are a magnificent person, and I salute you.

When it comes to dressing, there are broadly three options, and variants thereon. We'll look at them individually in a minute.

PUTTING AWAY CHILDISH THINGS

One of the perplexing things about ageing and how you look is the idea that, at some point, the things you like and love to wear are somehow no longer 'appropriate'. For example, in the summer I like to wear a shortish sundress and sandals. I have worn a shortish sundress and sandals every summer of my life, since round about toddlerhood. I have some nebulous notion about this not quite being the right look in middle age. (Why, though? Who says?) But in the absence of an alternative that ticks all the boxes – feels nice, looks nice, is cool (as in airy), is easy, aids leg-tanning, is a cinch to pack – my sundress and sandals are just what I wear. The question is, am I supposed to have some sort of age-related personality transplant at some point, and when does it come – at forty, fifty, sixty, seventy? My sandals make me happy, so how can they be sad? But maybe they *are* sad, in that I see them being worn by women three decades younger than me.

Is there a cut-off point? And how are you supposed to know what it is?

WOMAN NUMBER 1

You're the woman feasting in her onesie, not caring about stains. Let's call you Annie. When it comes to beauty and ageing, you do nothing. At all. You wither cheerfully, and spend your time doing more interesting things with your mind than fretting about, say, hair dye. You don't see it as withering, anyway. You see it as expanding – and perhaps you're right. You see this falling away of earthly vanities as a kind of liberation: at last, you are freed, and free. I take all my hats off to you. I also very humbly suggest the following.

To me, these are the absolute vanity basics – the bare minimum that even Don't Care Annie must take on board, not for reasons of 'duty' or anything else contentious, but for reasons of keeping and staying well. I would add 'dealing with facial hair' to this category, but I don't suppose Annie cares about a little tache – man, I am so not Annie – so I'll save it for later.

Feet

Freedom from cosmetic tyranny does not make one immune to the awful things that can happen to **feet**. The problem with feet is that once they're broken, they're pretty much impossible to fix. You're maybe not the kind of person who has regular pedicures, but do consider having occasional medical pedicures, which are more about

15

the nitty-gritty of chiropody than about cosmetic appeal (though there's overlap, obviously). For example, not caring about pedicures doesn't mean you have to develop hooves due to an over-abundance of hard skin – hard skin that then cracks, takes forever to heal and becomes agony to walk on. Who needs that? Equally, 'just' an ingrown toenail doesn't mean you just leave it or just live with the discomfort it causes.

NB: Foot pain can be a sign of gout. Please get it seen to, because it doesn't end well. Feet get knackered, and as far as I'm concerned anyone over the age of forty-five who doesn't develop almost obsessive foot vigilance is being short-sighted and foolish. Do you want to hobble around at some point in the future? Do you want to condemn yourself to twenty years of hideous, orthopaedic shoes? No. You do not.

* **In London, the queen of the medical pedicure is Margaret Dabbs,**[4] which I realize isn't much use if you don't live there, but I don't like recommending people I haven't been to personally. Ask around: there'll be someone good in your area. And don't dismiss the good old-fashioned chiropodist, either. They may lack glamour but they know their onions – or feet. The Society of Chiropodists and Podiatrists and the Institute of Chiropodists and Podiatrists

[4] margaretdabbs.co.uk

both have a facility on their websites to help you find the nearest accredited person.[5]

* **Marks & Spencer do the best foot file** – it's called Miracle Foot File and it's amazing, plus it's under a fiver and lasts forever. If you want a gadget that involves no elbow grease, you want the Micro-Pedi by Emjoi. It's battery operated and it gets every last bit of hard skin off in the most disgustingly satisfying way. Whatever you use, don't get carried away: that can be agony, too.

Last foot thing: never, ever ignore foot pain or foot weirdness. Not to freak you out or anything – swollen feet can just be swollen feet – but they can also, if they appear all of a sudden, indicate heart failure. If your feet feel numb, this can be a sign of really quite advanced diabetes, and that can end up with amputation. Obviously most instances of 'my feet are being weird' end up absolutely fine, and nobody whizzes you in to chop 'em off, but don't ever just 'leave it for a couple of days' when it comes to feet. FOOT VIGILANCE, that's what I say. At all times.

As well as feet, it is absolute folly to ignore **teeth**, and oral health in general. I have a fixation with teeth; keep reading for more later (or skip to page 186).

---

[5] scpod.org and iocp.org.uk

Eyes

Equally, you don't 'just' have to live with deteriorating **eyesight**. My life changed overnight when I had my short sight and astigmatism corrected at Moorfields Eye Hospital in London. The procedure, which I'd ignored for years due to fear – terror, really – and squeamishness, took minutes. If you want a minutely detailed account of the procedure, you will find it at the back of this book, on page 313. If you are considering or are curious about this, or any other corrective eye surgery, please read that account.

Do not, whatever you do, go and have it done for cheap on your local high street. Having dramatic things done for cheap on your local high street seldom ends well – as my friend who went and got her eyeliner tattooed on one day, because she was bored and it was on special offer, would attest. (It faded. Eventually.)

Also, most people our age eventually need reading glasses. Do yourself a favour and go get your eyes tested, then buy proper glasses for your particular prescription. Those cheap ones in the chemist's are only approximate, and their narrow frames are not universally flattering. You wouldn't wear an item of clothing that only fitted a bit: get proper specs.

Hair

If you've chosen to go grey, or indeed white, then you will know that the texture of your

hair has altered. Here are some important notes:

* **Lots of people think their grey hair is coarser.** This is not true. It is finer – all hair is, as we age – but it's not as well lubricated, due to lack of sebum (our oil glands produce less), so it can feel more straw-like. Don't make the common mistake of changing your shampoo to one for coarser, i.e. thicker, hair: the product will be too heavy and will make your fine hair seem limper and flatter. Instead, use a volumizing shampoo for fine hair.

  Also, there is no need to wash hair every day (unless you work on a construction site or similar). We're not *that* dirty. The reason your hair often looks better, and is easier to manage, a day or two after you've washed it is that the natural oils it contains have made their way back down the shaft, adding elasticity and improving texture. We all used to wash our hair once a week as children, and our hair was lovely because we didn't strip it every day. Don't over-wash it: it's especially unhelpful once you start going grey.

* **Your grey hair is also more susceptible to sun damage,** because of depleted melanin. Therefore, use a hair product containing SPF when you're in the sun – I like Kérastase Soleil's brilliant CC Crème, but loads of

different ones exist. Philip Kingsley's Elasticizer is an excellent treatment or mask. If you swim a lot, or are planning a beach holiday, his Swimcap cream will protect your hair from chlorine and salt water as well as from UV rays.

* **If you style your hair heavily, using dryers, irons, curlers, and so on,** then you must use something to protect it first, otherwise the coarseness problem will get completely out of hand (try Potion 9 by Sebastian, a brilliant all-rounder).

* **There is a colour-specific line of shampoos and conditioners,** which you may also want to take a look at. Again, I can highly recommend them, having farmed them out to several guinea pigs. The range is called White Hot Hair and details are on their website.[6]

WOMAN NUMBER 2

Now, let's look at the second option: Woman Number 2. She does a little bit. She's not going to go nuts over the whole business, but she likes the idea of looking as good as she can without going overboard. She's most of us, I think. Let's call her Sophie.

[6] whitehothair.co.uk

Teeth

First, teeth. NOTHING IS AS AGEING AS HAVING RUBBISH TEETH. Equally, nothing has as much of a youthifying effect as a mouth that's in excellent nick, or as close as. This fact is the very foundation of 'older' beauty, plus it's one of the things you can do that makes everybody think you look 'well' and, in some cases, dramatically better. If your teeth weren't great, and are suddenly much improved, people will scour your face in a puzzled-seeming way, trying to fathom out what you've had done. Sometimes they suspect Botox-like trickery or surgical intervention. But it's not – it's only teeth. I call this a highly satisfactory result.

So let's talk about teeth. We may be some time, because I'm quite evangelical on this topic. This is going to sound incredibly simple, but: **white teeth**. Whiter teeth, at any rate. I'm not going to suggest you remortgage the house and go and get a mouthful of veneers – a very extreme and problematical course of action (they fall off all the time, basically, revealing the creepy little roughed-up stumps below) that I'd only suggest if your teeth are really an absolute abomination. Few people's are, because we're not medieval peasants. Of course, if we were medieval peasants, we'd either be dead before we reached middle age or be known throughout the hamlet as Old Nan or The Crone. Bleak times.

I wouldn't get too hung up on **crookedness**, either, because slightly crooked teeth are charming and characterful. Also, you have to be very careful with sudden, dramatic mouth overhauls. At our age, absolutely perfect teeth – giant, square, fluorescent-white veneers – look startling in the extreme but also, more to the point, ageing. That's because you've got a teenage Miami cheerleader's teeth in your 55-year-old face. This causes the onlooker to think, 'Something's wrong here, and it's not the teeth – those teeth are immaculate and amazing. So it must be the face. Oh yes! The face is really old and doesn't match the teeth.' People will think this even if the face isn't 'really old' and merely middle-aged, because the frickin' teeth emphasize the contrast so cruelly. So leave well alone. It doesn't matter that your teeth are crooked.

Whitening, though: now you're talking (and smiling. Beaming! So cheering, and transformative).

* **Making your teeth significantly whiter, by yourself, at home, is easy.** You need a top-of-the-range electric toothbrush. I'm afraid these aren't cheap – the Philips Sonicare range, which is the one I recommend, starts from £50 and skyrockets upwards from there – so ask for one for Christmas. However, used in conjunction with a safe whitening toothpaste (I recommend the Janina brand), you basically get a whole new mouth in about three weeks.

Chuck in a Sonicare AirFloss, a terrifyingly effective device that blasts every iota of plaque into oblivion (and on to your bathroom mirror – stand well back), and you're practically Miss Teeth of the Year. NB: The AirFloss was called the BloodFloss in my house when I first got one; it passes.

* **Your dental hygienist will dispose of staining caused by tea, red wine, tobacco and the like;** the Sonicare will subsequently keep it at bay (but do keep visiting your hygienist regularly, not least because a load of health problems manifest themselves via the mouth and gums – sinister but true, which is why even people with dentures need to go and see the dentist).

* **The best and fastest way of getting dramatically whiter teeth** is by spending a couple of hours a week wearing made-to-measure bleaching trays. See your dentist. They cost from about £250 and last forever. Don't use those cheap, ready-made ones: they aren't moulded to your own teeth and there-fore merrily leak peroxide down your throat, which on balance you can probably do without.

It's a fact that **enamel thins** as we get older, which can lead to all sorts of problems. There are several new toothpastes that claim to reverse this and to actually rebuild enamel. Of the ones I've tried, the most impressive is called Regenerate and is made by Unilever (which I mention only because those huge companies have huge amounts of money to spend on research – they therefore tend not to make false claims).

Haircut

Next, Sophie needs **a good haircut**. Not a decent haircut, not an OK haircut, not her 'trademark' haircut that she's had since she was twenty: no, a good, a *really good* haircut that works perfectly for this precise time of life. You can see what the problem is here: exceptional, life-changing hair-cuts are rarer than hen's teeth, and this isn't *Honey* magazine in 1983 (more's the pity), so I'm not going to tell you how to have a conver-sation with your hairdresser. I do have some tips, though.

Hair is such an emotive subject, and the way we feel about our hair is not rational. Yes, it's only hair. It's also an expression of femininity, it's sexy, it's supposed to be our 'crowning glory' and it's tied in very closely with how we feel we look – we don't have 'bad mascara' days, or 'crap tights' days,[7] only bad hair ones. It follows that

[7] Actually, I totally have crap tights days (best opaque tights: M&S Autograph Velvet Touch – Lords of Tights, Princes of Hosiery).

anything that happens to our hair that we can't control – any age-related changes in texture or volume, for instance – can feel absolutely devastating, and that's before you get to *really* upsetting things like hair loss or alopecia. (If you're losing a really alarming amount of hair – losing a fair bit is completely normal – then do have your thyroid function checked.) While I'm at it with hair loss and alopecia: if braving it out is not for you and the idea of wigs makes you want to cry, please be aware that there are absolutely amazing wigs out there these days, and they are the least wiggy wigs imaginable. You can swim and shower in them, and drive an open-top car in a gale. They look completely natural and you honestly, truly, can't tell they're a wig, even if you get really close up to the wearer and stare and stare (I have done this). You always used to be able to tell from the hairline: wigs, even expensive wigs, have a sort of solid, neatly demarcated line at the front. Nobody's hairline does this naturally, unless you're a supercool young black guy who's shaved his into a neat strip. So, two choices:

* **Make like an African-American superstar** and go for a 'lace-front' wig, where the front part of the wig is gauze-like and has individual hairs positioned to resemble a true and natural hairline. These wigs can face any wind machine/force 10 gale. Catwalk Beauty in Brixton, London, has an impressive selection.

25

* **If you want to go less pop star and more normal person,** you want something called vacuum real-hair wigs ('Man, the terminology is sexy,' says the wig-wearing friend who got me on to these) – see Positively Hair's website[8] for all information. They use human hair and take a mould of your head to ensure a perfect fit. The wigs do not ever come off accidentally, due to the vacuum business. They are fantastic.

You have to bite the bullet, with hair. You have to be brave and unflinching and look in the mirror and ask yourself some unpleasant questions, and then you have to make what David Cameron would call 'tough decisions'.

Now, you can stop reading this bit if your hair is indeed your crowning glory. If it's the hair you had at twenty-one – as lush, as thick, as corn-coloured, falling to your shoulders in Botticelli waves – then hurrah. Before you go off and have a jubilant cup of tea, though, just quickly ask yourself if you're happy with its cut, and with its length.

Hopefully, the answer will be yes. But I'm just quickly going to point a few things out like an insistent spoilsport:

* **Your 'signature cut' may not actually be the best cut for you in middle age** – not because it doesn't look nice, but because,

8 positivelyhair.co.uk

oddly, having the same cut for twenty or thirty years can be immensely ageing in itself. It's back to my teeth example above. Someone looks at you – someone who's known you since forever. 'Ah,' they say to themselves, 'here's lovely Sophie. She has the hair she had when I first met her at that party in 1985 – that gorgeous hair. It's exactly the same. Same cut, same colour, same everything. God, it takes me back. And here's Sophie's dear face and it looks exac— Oh, Christ. Well, never mind. We all get older. I'm hardly an oil painting myself, these days.' And this is the **hair/face dichotomy**. You may not mind it, but you should be aware that it exists, and that there exists an alternative scenario, where the person is going, 'Ah, lovely Sophie. She looks great,' without detouring into a whole tragic hair cul-de-sac. So bear that in mind.

* **Beware the perils of long hair.** It used to be thought, absurdly, that long hair on a woman past forty was somehow unseemly. And then people evolved, thank God, and now of course you can have whatever length of hair you like. Actually, I say that – I'm very against Pointlessly Long Hair on anyone, but especially on the middle-aged. This is a personal prejudice, though, so do ignore me – except it's so creepy, Pointlessly Long Hair. Who do those women with thinning waist-length hair

think they are – a mermaid? A princess? You know – at *fifty*? Gosh.

* **I am also against Pointlessly Short Hair.** Pointlessly Short Hair is absolutely beautiful when it works, but *unbelievably* unforgiving when it doesn't. You need a thin pointy-featured face – quite like an elf's, actually – an impeccably firm jawline, great skin and very good bone structure, so that you're mostly cheekbones and eyes as opposed to, for instance, chin and nose. In middle age, this is very much not a given, simply because with the best will in the world it's hard (but not impossible) to be gamine when you have grandchildren. There was a time when every woman over forty had Pointlessly Short Hair, and it made me sad – automatic short hair, plus nan-clothes, were what made those women inescapably dowdy, like giving children with Down's syndrome bowl haircuts in the 1970s, as though that was just the way their hair grew: what stupid madness. Where women can manage it, though – the gamine crop, not the bowl – it's sensational. Also, congratulations: you're Jane Birkin.

* **Most of us do better with something in-between** – and, as I say, I am a great believer in having new hair every few years, and in not letting things stagnate. This happens

best if your hairdresser's sense of style errs on the side of the classical. There's a certain look some middle-aged women have, which says, not unpoignantly, 'My 26-year-old hairdresser is my friend and really understands the inner me, the Fun Me trying to get out, and together we express the Fun Me through my hair.' I am not a fan of the Fun Me. People on the Tube don't go, 'Aw, look, she's really a fun person.' They go, 'All right, Su Pollard?'

MATCHING THE BACK TO THE FRONT

My point about long hair is this: you look completely different from the back than you do from the front. Of course, there are lots of ways in which this happens anyway – you may have the gait of a sprightly gazelle or impala at sixty-eight, you may have the enviable figure of a teenager, you may be wearing Daisy Dukes (please don't be wearing Daisy Dukes).

Recently, a man followed me down Greek Street in Soho, all the way to Soho Square. I was coming out of a shop. Eventually he caught up with me and said, to my back, 'I can never resist a hot brunette,' which I thought was not un-charming – in a 'or possibly it's quite creepy' way. Anyway, I turned round to say something and saw that the man was in his early thirties, tops (I could technically have given birth to him). Clearly unable to self-edit his speech, he said, 'Oh . . . no, it's still OK.'

Put it this way: I nearly died during that ellipsis. Imagine if he'd said 'Oh . . . my mistake' or 'Oh . . . sorry, ma'am' or just 'Oh . . . JESUS CHRIST'. I mean, it must happen, and I think it's a lot more likely to happen if your hair is longer and therefore younger-looking. Because what made me a 'hot brunette' was my hair (shoulder-length).

Beware. It can look lovely, but it can also look very mutton.

Still on hair: staying blonde is easy, staying dark is hard. If you have – or had – really dark hair to start off with, be extremely wary of trying to keep it that way: it doesn't work. Dyed black hair looks blocky and wig-like, no matter how skilled the technician. Go darkest, most bitter brown instead (a kind of 80 per cent cocoa solids shade is what you're aiming for), and whack some highlights in there to light your face up. Nothing is less flattering to skin than that harsh blue-black colour (this also applies to clothes, as we shall see), unless you're Chinese or Japanese and your blue-black hair is real.

If you want to try out a new shade or hairstyle, bear the following in mind:

* **Never, ever go to a new hairdresser for a dramatic change** – of cut or colour, but especially cut.

* **Tearing pictures out of magazines is still a good idea** – or rather, doing a Google image search on your iPad and presenting it to the hairdresser like an offering, or like a cat with a dead bird. A good hairdresser will be blunt and say no if the cut you're thinking of is wrong. Never mind your fat-faced hurt feelings – be grateful.

* **There's nothing wrong with stopping women in the street and saying,** 'Excuse me, where did you get your hair cut?' especially if the woman's hair is similar to yours.

* **There is nothing wrong, either, with trying on wigs** – especially if you're going from long to short.

This is a contentious thing to say, but it may be that the thing your husband/boyfriend/partner likes best about you is your current hair. He's an arse in this respect, obviously, because what he should like best is YOU, not a load of strands of stupid keratin. Nevertheless, there are few things more crushing than coming home with a radical change and seeing the face of someone you love fall sadly to the ground – and to be fair to husbands/

31

partners, I'd be very sad if mine suddenly grew an enormous Gandalf beard. If you're living with, or involved with, some hair fanatic, take soundings first. It ought to be perfectly possible to agree on something that everybody's happy with.

However, having said that, the excuse 'my husband likes it this way' is responsible for 90 per cent of beauty, hair and sartorial horrors. Your husband may really like you butt-naked and smoking a cheroot, but there's a time and a place. It's your hair. Be the boss of it.[9]

WOMAN NUMBER 3

Then there's Woman Number 3, and she's having no truck with any of this mimsy bullshit. She is simply not having it. In a way she's as magnificent as Woman Number 1, with her diametrically opposed but equally spirited *refusal*. No, she says. No, no, no, *no*. I know I can't ultimately stop any of this happening, but I am going to do everything in my power to delay decrepitude for as long as I can.

Woman Number 3 – let's call her Esmeralda – gets a hard time. I sometimes think that Woman Number 2, Sophie – who occupies broadly the same territory as many of us – is a bit of a weed. She's sitting on the fence when it comes to beauty

[9] I have never had a bad cut at John Frieda. It is fair to say that John Frieda changed my hair life.

32

and age: on the one hand, yes, I'll get an expensive, really good haircut; on the other hand, God, no, I'd never have fillers – what kind of a person do you take me for? This only really works intellectually up to a point. For example, if Sophie has naturally great hair and is spending an actually quite pointless fortune on it, wouldn't the money be better spent on fixing the massive crevasse-sized wrinkle between her brows? And yet Esmeralda is the one we all sit in judgement on. How shallow she must be. How vain. How tragic, ultimately, to set so much value on delaying the inevitable. This is terribly hypocritical. Who hasn't been curious about Botox, or fillers, or the idea of hoiking everything up just a teeny bit?

The real question here is, who does it hurt? And the answer is complicated: at one level, it hurts absolutely nobody. Esmeralda's got her fillers and her new tits, and she's as happy as a clam. What's it to you? At another level, though, it hurts – so the argument goes – all of us. It hurts those of us who are left behind, wrinkly and slack-bosomed,[10] because it lets the side down. Because of women like Esmeralda, the idea of what a woman of forty, or fifty, or sixty 'should' look like has shifted – whoosh – *wayyyyy* over there, where it's hard to keep up. And that doesn't make us feel good, and

[10] Indignant footnote: I am not slack-bosomed. I *am* quite slack-stomached, but it seems an OK price to pay for three bouncing, giant children.

so we look for someone to blame. 'Look here, Esmeralda,' we say, 'it's hard enough living in a society that places so little value on middle-aged women without you swanning about, with a face that's as smooth as an egg and with rock-hard 36Ds.' You're not very *sisterly*, Esmo, and that is bad. So we will now make all sorts of assumptions about you – about your intellect, what you're like as a person, even about your capabilities as a mother. These assumptions will not be flattering.

This, in itself, is of course a very *unsisterly* response. We're in six-kettles-and-half-a-dozen-pots territory here. Let's not forget that even Woman Number 1, with her gnarly feet and her gigantic smock, sits in judgement on Women Numbers 2 and 3: she thinks they're not just silly but unforgivably so for concerning themselves with this stuff; by extension, she thinks she's *cleverer*. The cleverest, in fact. I hate to break it to Woman Number 1, but sitting in Birkenstocks reading Jung and ignoring your gross feet does not make you the intellectual superior of the other two – not even of Esmeralda, who, for all you know, is a thoracic surgeon.

SISTERS UNDER THE SKIN

The truth of the matter is, we're all a composite of those three types of women.

And so I think we should focus on our similarities, not our differences, and I think we should cut other women some slack. It's all very well spending your energies on going, 'But I want to be better looking/more fanciable/sexier/better dressed/in better nick than her, and her, and her,' but it really doesn't get you anywhere, plus pointless anxiety is really bad for the skin (fact, not exaggeration – so is stress. It's to do with cortisol levels – see page 309 for more). Also, these anxieties are embarrassingly teenaged, given that we're grown-ups. So here is some general beauty advice, hard-earned, for you in middle age and upwards, regardless of what type of person you consider yourself to be. You're allowed to flit between the categories – we all do. If we admitted it – if we were cool with being gnarly-footed one day and 'toxed up the next – and if we saw no insurmountable contradictions in it, we'd all be a fat lot happier. So:

1. **Everything you think about Botox is wrong.**
   People always say, 'Oh my God, she's had such bad Botox.' Bad Botox – the rigid forehead, the shine, the egg look – has come to define the way we view Botox, which is nuts. The whole *point* of good Botox is that you don't notice it. The person just looks better, brighter, perkier, in a hard-to-pin-down way. Ergo, nobody ever says, 'She's had great Botox,' because if it's great, you won't know about it. There are lots and *lots* of people walking around with amazing Botox – you just don't know it's there. And note: these people are often the

ones who look completely natural and wear very little, if any, make-up; the ones of whom you think, 'She just has amazing genes.' Dissing Botox is like saying, 'Oh my God, pencil skirts are awful,' because the only ones you've ever seen are made of nylon and slit to the arse. Botox can be absolutely fantastic, and absolutely awful. A good practitioner will explain the risks to you.

All of this also applies to injectables, though these require additional caution because many last for years rather than months, and if you don't like the effect, you're buggered. For both, and for dermatological improvements generally, I highly recommend Dr Frances Prenna Jones,[11] who I go to myself – not too often, because that way madness lies. Prices are, as you'd expect, not cheap. Because it's your face. She also has her own minimalist range of hyper-efficient products, which I rate very highly.

2. **Less is more.** It may seem counter-intuitive, but the older you get, the less make-up you need. But the make-up that you do need must be absolutely top notch – you're too old to be wasting time and money on old-fashioned formulas, or stuff that slides off or cakes or doesn't make a dramatic difference. If your

[11] drfrancesprennajones.com. She is currently having a new website designed as this book goes to press.

make-up bag is full of old bits of tat and broken blusher cases, dump it and start again. I write a beauty column in the *Sunday Times* and get sent a lot of samples. But when I buy my own make-up, with my own money, the brands I use are Armani, Bobbi Brown, Charlotte Tilbury and MAC. This isn't to say that other brands aren't brilliant, because lots of them are. But if you want make-up that works, that is flattering, that stays put and that basically does the business, they're a good place to start. Also, they're reliable: they're good across the board, unlike many brands who do an amazing this and a fantastic that but a crap third thing.

As a bonus, all four of these brands do really excellent in-store makeovers; MAC does specific, affordable classes that are genius if you are, say, a person who's never understood how to put on eyeshadow properly. (These classes make excellent presents. Knowing how to put make-up on for maximum effect is an invaluable skill – it's like magic: suddenly piggy-eyed little you is like something from anime. It's *never* too late to learn how to do your make-up brilliantly, and the classes are not expensive.)

3. **Good skin is the most important thing.** For me, Armani's foundations are second to none – specifically Maestro Fusion, which has the texture of water and is the ultimate foundation for people who normally hate

foundation – but all of the above brands have exceptional offerings. Tinted moisturizers: Guerlain first, then Laura Mercier and Nars. Also, buy yourself a Clarisonic facial cleansing brush, the single best thing you can do for your skin. See also mineral foundation.

4. **If your eyes look fantastic, the rest of your face can handle any number of imperfections.** This is a neat trick. Learn to perfect your eye make-up and your beauty life is instantly simplified. Again, it's all in the tools. The brands above have excellent pencils and shadows, as does By Terry (amazing pencils). The easiest way of learning new techniques is to go online and find some good make-up tutorials. I like Lisa Eldridge's,[12] which are clear and easy to follow, but see my earlier point about in-store classes.

5. **Blusher can take years off.** Mad sort of beauty-speak thing to say, but true. Do a big, exaggerated fake smile and apply blusher on the fat bits of the cheeks – the apples – rather than sucking in your face and applying it to the hollows (very eighties – your lipstick is no longer called Iron Lady or Copper Knockers). Use fingers or a small brush: those huge fluffy ones aren't nearly precise enough.

[12] lisaelridge.com

Armani's Cheek Fabric Blush in shade 506 looks amazing on everybody who is from very white to Asian/mid-brown. If your skin is very dry, cream blusher may be a better idea. Try cream eyeshadow too – though remember that all cream or all powder will not last as long as a mixture: powder shadow will last longer if it has something to stick to (such as a cream primer), and so on.

6. **Discover the benefits of contouring.** If you're good with a brush, you can now suck in your cheeks and, with a very light hand, use a contouring powder (good ones are a really ugly, muddy dirty-brown colour) in the hollows and under your chin. Contouring is highly fashionable as I write, because it can have amazing results. Do practise, though. It can also look like your face has got strange mud-coloured stripes on it. Also, save it for the evening: it works best in forgiving light.

7. **Have a look at Studio 10.** This is a small line developed by Grace Fodor[13] with the middle-aged and upwards specifically in mind. The products are brilliant, pared down and simplified, and idiot-proof. She does a particularly good, hard-to-mess-up contour kit, as per point 6 above.

[13] studio10beauty.com

8. **Shine sits in creases.** Avoid this by using an eye primer (I like Urban Decay's), which will smooth out the entire area and prolong the staying power of the product. Go easy with deliberate shine on the rest of the face, while not shunning it entirely (shine restores youthful bloom; going super-matte can make you look quite desiccated).

9. **Buy a new mascara.** The most recent formulations come pretty close to looking like eyelash extensions (special mention to Charlotte Tilbury's Full Fat Lashes and to MAC's 3D Black Lash). When it comes to everyday make-up, I think that as you age a good rule of thumb is to up the mascara and go easier on the liner – it gives wide eyes, rather than sharply delineated ones, and is much more youthful-looking and flattering. For the same reason, liner often looks better smudged – or use shadow.

10. **The rule for eyeshadows and liners involves the colour wheel:** if you want your eyes to 'pop' (eyes 'popping' always reminds me of aged colonels spluttering with disgust), then you want to use the colour that's opposite yours on the wheel: brown, rusty shades for blue eyes, purples for green eyes, and so on. It's not an immutable rule, obviously

– wear what you like – but it's handy to bear in mind if you want maximum emphasis.

11. **Maintain good eyebrows.** These work like a mini facelift, because everything gets hoiked upwards. If years of plucking have left yours too sparse, or if you have alopecia, Sophie Thorpe[14] will tattoo you some semi-permanent new ones. I realize this may sound alarming, but there's no need for fear – she's brilliant (and expensive, I'm afraid). If your eyebrows are still in good nick, threading gives a neater effect than plucking and is faster and less painful.

12. **Invest in decent skincare.** I could write an entire book about this subject alone. However, in the absence of space – and if you don't care about products not looking particularly glamorous, as long as they really work – Bioderma has a range for every skin type, is not expensive and the entire range is extremely effective.

13. **Crème de la Mer.** The answer to, 'Is Crème de la Mer worth it?' – everyone always asks – is, 'Yes, very much so, but only if you are forty plus and your skin is normal to dry.' There's a lighter lotion that's better for oilier

14 sophiethorpe.co.uk

skin. The whole range is phenomenal, to be honest – eye-watering price tag and all.

14. **If you buy one expensive thing, make it a top-notch moisturizer.** Keeping your skin moist prevents lines and wrinkles. Thirsty skin looks knackered, which is the opposite of what you want.

15. **Go easy on exfoliation.** That includes both scrubbing at your face with grainy products and using skincare that contains acids. They work beautifully, but they thin the skin over time. For every day, just use your preferred cleanser and a hot flannel, which will exfoliate gently without doing damage.

16. **Clichéd but true.** After a certain age, it's your arse or your face. Go for the face. Don't starve yourself: being too thin can be unbelievably ageing. Fat fills out wrinkles; being a bit too fat is more flattering than being a bit too thin. Think of it as nature's injectable fillers.

17. **Eye creams are not worth it.** Just use your normal moisturizer, in minuscule doses, and pat it on using your ring finger[15] rather than

[15] Because you instinctively use your ring finger much

rubbing it in (the skin here is unbelievably delicate). A top cosmetic surgeon once told me a really revolting story about people having 'pouches of fatty deposit' under the eyes as a result of using too much eye cream. If you have huge, pouchy bags under your eyes, know that blepharoplasty (the surgery to remove these) is extremely effective, makes a huge difference, is uncomplicated and straightforward, and you can usually go home the same day.

18. **Some night creams are worth it.** But see above: your normal moisturizer will work, too. If you're very dry, oils work even better (I love Decléor's). If you're oily, you don't need a night cream. Save your money.

19. **Top tip if you're oily (which is really frickin' annoying beyond the age of fourteen):** try Bioderma's Sébium range. Also, cheer up: oily skin ages more slowly because it remains relatively lubricated and therefore elastic.

20. **In my view, the best concealers are:** Secret Camouflage by Laura Mercier – which will cover pretty much anything you want covered without looking cakey or obvious – and The

---

more lightly and delicately than your great big battering-ram index finger.

Retoucher by Charlotte Tilbury – which is creamier and comes in a Touche Éclat-style pen. It's better than any others at erasing shadows under the eyes.

21. **Always use a sunscreen.** No, this isn't glossy-magazine guff. Brown spots are to be avoided, as are wrinkles. Save yourself. Put it on the backs of your hands as well as on your face. Daily sunscreens these days are not claggy and zincy, and nor will they make you look like a ghost. Alpha-H, an Australian brand that, being Australian, really understands about sun damage, does a brilliant Daily Essential Moisturizer with SPF30 as part of its comprehensive range.

22. **You can't get rid of proper, deep wrinkles with anything you buy over the counter.** You can get rid of them, or soften them dramatically, with injectables. Be careful, though. A face that is entirely unlined is Humpty Dumpty's face. If you're going down this route, inject the crevasses, leave the rest, i.e. the smaller wrinkles, alone. As an adult, a completely smooth face is a face that's never laughed or cried. It is not attractive.

23. **Don't ignore your neck.** Necks have the terrible habit of looking perfectly normal and

44

then suddenly going all chicken-necky in the space of about two weeks, something that is irreversible. Use whatever you're using on your face on your neck too, to prevent this, plus whack on the sunscreen here (a medium to high factor) – neck skin is very thin and needs extra protection.

24. **Lip fillers look awful on everyone.** Where they don't look awful, they look off-puttingly sore, as if they might crack and start seeping. Charlotte Tilbury does a brilliant skin-coloured (if you're white to mid-brown) pencil that allows you to effortlessly cheat your natural lip shape, should you wish to do so.

25. **Crêpey cleavage is not a great look.** It's nice to be proud of your bosom – but wear something figure-hugging rather than a deep V. There's nothing you can do to de-crêpe the cleavage. Sorry. This is why **staying out of the sun** would have been a good idea twenty years ago. Still, I'd rather someone was crêpey than know that they spent decades sitting under a parasol slathered in factor 50 and wearing a huge hat, looking pained. You have to seize the pleasure of the moment, sometimes. Use sunblock from now on, though.

26. **Hands show your age** (there are mad cosmetic procedures to tackle this – but who

has the time or the money, really?). Carry hand cream with you; if your hands look knackered, short square nails are better than talons (who still has talons? Cool fifteen-year-olds from Dalston. Not you, I hope).

27. **Drink water, and plenty of it.** By the time you register thirst, you are already mildly dehydrated. Don't be dehydrated, it's withering.

28. **Get online and look up the benefits of coconut oil** (it needs to be virgin and raw; mine is by Biona and I get it cheap at the supermarket) both applied topically and ingested. It's pretty amazing stuff. It's powerfully antibacterial and antifungal, due to containing a very high proportion of something called lauric acid (it clears up rashes like billy-o, including on pets).

If you look it up, you will see that people make fairly extraordinary claims about it, including the unproven assertion that it helps with Alzheimer's and cholesterol. I don't know about that, but: it makes a great cleanser if your skin is very dry; it's a great eye make-up remover; it heals damaged skin freakishly fast; it tames a frizzy barnet; it's a brilliant hair treatment (whack a nut-sized lump on, sit and watch telly, wash it out after twenty minutes); it gives a lovely gloss to limbs. There really are dozens of uses. And, obviously, you can also cook with it: it's incredibly good for you, and it tastes delicious.

29. **Do yoga.** I realize that this seems like an arbitrary sort of admonition, but I really mean it. Everyone I know who's over fifty and looks fantastic – including one woman well into her early eighties – does yoga. Just do yoga. You can thank me later.

PS: Be very, very careful of running. I don't care what anyone says, my GP and I are agreed that it *always* buggers your knees in the end.

CHAPTER 2

WHAT TO WEAR

Or what not to wear, and the fear of mutton

First things first: as I was saying in the previous chapter, don't get too thin. I know that seems mad, when much of women's youth is spent trying to be skinny, something that involves varying degrees of deprivation, self-loathing and actual insanity. But remember:

* **What was fashionably thin in your late thirties does not necessarily translate well into your late forties and beyond** – unless, of course, you are one of those women who eats like a horse and is naturally rake thin.

* **Being too thin, as in unnaturally thin, makes you look frailer** – not damsel-in-distress, I'm-so-pretty-and-weak frail (though why anyone would want to look like that beats me) but like-an-old-woman frail, osteoporosis frail, body-failing-me frail.

* **If you're too thin, you'll have a scrawny neck.** Nobody wants that.

* **Being too thin shows up every line and wrinkle** – and it can end up looking quite monkey-like. If you want to look less wrinkly, put some weight on.

On the other hand, don't get too fat. Your body is doing the best it can, several decades in, but let's not take the piss. It can only work with what you give it, and if what you give it causes thigh-rub and squashed feet, it may be time for a change. Think of your body as a beautiful vintage Mustang – it goes like the clappers provided you don't clog it up with weird stuff. If you're too fat, cut the carbs and the sugar. That's it. Do those two things and you will lose weight.

Next: nobody over the age of forty can get away with doing absolutely no exercise. At the very least, walk, slightly faster than is comfortable, and for as long as you can manage without turning up at the office covered in sweat. There's no point in telling people who don't like exercise to join a class or a gym (I should know – I am that person), but here again I say to you: yoga. Just do yoga, and everything will be fine.

Now, clothes:

* Can you shop at Topshop?
* Can you wear leopard print?

★   Can you wear fishnets, ripped jeans, stupid, impractical shoes?

Yes, yes, yes, though perhaps not all at the same time. But read on – I'm going to get quite specific.

FASHION IS A TYRANNY

It's a benign despot – it's jolly, and it's fun, and it's creative and interesting; it can even be art. Nevertheless, it *is* a tyranny. And it is pathetic – in the true sense of arousing pity through vulnerability – to continue to bow to that tyranny when you are a mature adult who is considerably closer to old age than she is to teenagehood. By slavishly following fashion, you can make yourself faintly ridiculous. That's because fashion is not made for you. It's made for young people. You may as well slavishly follow skate-boarding trends. You know – do it, if it makes you happy. Do it – you don't need telling by me – if your business in life has always involved fashion. If you're anybody else, though – if you're the woman who stands in a department store and says, 'I have no idea about fashion any more; I don't know what to buy!' with panic in her voice – be aware that you no longer have any need to be under the yoke.

You are free. You can wear what you like, what suits you, what you're comfortable in, regardless of what magazines are telling you to wear. And then nobody will look at your sixty-year-old self, proudly decked out top to toe in this season's latest, and think, 'Aw, bless.'

STYLE MATTERS

Fashion may increasingly feel like an irrelevance, but style is everything. It's also individual and often innate, but here are some useful pointers:

* **If you're happy wearing it and it makes you feel good,** chances are that you look fantastic, whether it's a gardening outfit or a smart dress. Eighty per cent of looking good is confidence.

* **You're old enough,** or should be, to have fathomed out what suits you and what doesn't. Go with that instinct. On the other hand, you're also old enough to be set in your ways, and that may not necessarily be a good thing, sartorially. For example, I have lived – lived, I tell you – by the decree that having big tits meant a normal-necked garment would result in catastrophe. For decades, I only wore U-necks or V-necks. It turns out that this isn't true: provided the garment is fitted and not flowing or loose, a normal neck can work very well. I learned this aged forty-five. So keep an open mind, and if a friend or sales assistant (or a part of your own brain) says, 'Hey, why

51

not try this?' don't automatically discount the suggestion. Also, bodies change. Also, you might want to change the focus of emphasis as the years pass.

* **Never buy anything too small,** on the basis that you'll slim your way into it. You won't, and it's depressing.

* **There's actually no such thing as 'too young for me',** unless you're trying to squeeze yourself into children's clothing (and see below). Conversely, 'too old' very much exists, and dressing too old is a common mistake.

* **Role models:** we all have women whose style we admire, and that's a good thing. It can be very useful when you're dithering over buying something: 'Would so-and-so wear it?' you ask yourself, and it helps clarify matters. The thing is, make that person somebody who is roughly in your age bracket and who isn't your complete physical opposite. It's all very well admiring Alexa Chung, but it's not really going to butter any sartorial parsnips if you're fifty-five and tubby. Constantly comparing yourself to someone who is half your age and ultra-gorgeous is bad for morale, as well as utterly pointless. Pick a style role model that is realistic.

ENTERING THE WORLD OF 'OLDISH'

When you emerge from the Youngish Pastures into the world of Oldish, please be aware of the following:

* **Neutrals can be very ageing.** They're magnolia walls and a beige three-piece suite: the immediate effect is not one of verve and vitality but of something dull and uninteresting. 'But so classic,' you say, clinging to your beige, which you call 'camel' or 'buff'. I guess. I wouldn't call magnolia and beige 'classic', myself. More 'for people who last decorated in 1986'. Sticking to this interiors theme, if you're naturally cautious and prefer only a very little colour that won't frighten the horses, think Farrow & Ball shades rather than glaringly obvious Dulux, as it were (although Dulux the paint brand is brilliant and will match you any F&B colour. I'm just saying, don't wear Dulux clothes if colour scares you).

* **Black looks absolutely awful on almost everyone,** and the problem is exacerbated with every year that passes. It drains you and makes you look knackered. It's so stark that every imperfection is thrown into sharp relief. It's also very easy for black to look cheap. A really immaculate little black dress (expensive), fine. But that's about it. Never wear black if your hair's falling out – because it just sits there

on the fabric, looking depressing – or if you're clumsy and spill things down yourself.

* **Conversely, navy blue is universally flattering,** and it works regardless of skin tone or hair colouring. Navy is chic, grown-up, unshouty, but never funereal – and at this stage, we really don't want to be reminding ourselves, or anybody else, of Queen Victoria in mourning.

* **Grey is the colour of fog, pigeons and mice.** Why anyone older would want to wear it top to toe is a mystery (also, it's reminiscent of school uniforms, for which you're *too old*). NB: Grey looks especially unflattering against brown or black skin.

* **Neutrals are about hiding.** Don't hide. Why would you hide?

COLOUR IS *LIFE*

Things that are pleasing to the eye – flowers, seascapes, paintings, animals – are not monochrome, apart from zebras. Things that are depressing – mud, dirt, pollution, pavements, grime – are from the end of the colour spectrum that older women somehow often choose to wear.

For God's sake, wear colour – proper, beautiful colour. When I decided to write this book, I made two notes on the back of my hand. One said, ALWAYS SPEND THE MONEY ON TEETH, and the other said, COLOUR, FFS.

Colour is a feast for the eyes. Colour makes you feel happier – try having a brown kitchen, and then painting it pink – and it makes people who look at you feel less bummed-out and better disposed. Colour flatters the skin like nothing else, which is why when we put on make-up we put on colour (doh). Now, I'm not advocating top-to-toe colour, because then you might run the peril of looking WHACKY, which as far as I am concerned is simply the pits. The two great pitfalls of middle age and upwards, clothes-wise, are:

* WHACKY (aka Art Teacher With Cats, GSOH), *and*

* HAMPSTEAD LADY (aka I Love Culture, Me).

It's hard to know which is worse, really.

HOW TO AVOID WHACKY

- **You can wear 'fun' tights,** and you can wear clashing prints, and you can wear pod-like shoes from Scandinavia with red laces, but not all at the same time. You're a human being. You're not a laminated 'humorous' sign in an office.

- **Keep your spectacles a reasonable colour.** You like purple: great. So do I. But not plonked in the middle of your face, for whacky 'fun'.

- **Anything 'little girl' is sinister enough at any point past the age of seven,** but it's really, deeply creepy and unsettling in an older woman. No hair bobbles. No plaits – wotcha, Heidi – or bunches. No ankle socks, even if the ankle socks are on top of the fun tights. No gingham. No jelly sandals. No, not even those Vivienne Westwood ones made for Japanese teenagers. No Mary Janes. NB: Some sugary pastels can have this effect, too. If it makes you feel like you should have Sudocrem on your bottom and do a big, good burp for Mummy, take it back.

- **Vintage** – divine. But top-to-toe vintage from the eighties, when you were twenty-one – weird and sad. I think the rule is that you can do vintage from any time up until the decade just before your late teens/early twenties.

- **Fun jewellery** – a necklace made of plastic cherries, say: why not? Sometimes.

Against something sober and plain. Piled-on fun jewellery you like so much that you bought it in pineapple and banana too: perhaps not. Some people can carry this off, though. Just not very many.

- **Avoid anything made of wood** – for example, chunky earrings in the shape of parrots, or enormous noisy painted bangles.

- **Beware 'ethnic' clothing that does not belong to your particular ethnicity.** I can wear a sari and a bindi, should the mood take me. I'm not sure about you, just as you might not be sure about me wearing one of those enormous traditional Welsh hats at all times, even if it was 'out of respect for the culture'.

HOW TO AVOID HAMPSTEAD LADY

It's probably easier if I describe Hampstead Lady to you – that way you'll know how not to be her. Beware, though: even perfectly nice people turn into Hampstead Lady with the passage of time, because the HL look is so easy to pull together. It's very much a look – it gives the impression that you know what you're doing. Here's how (or rather, how not):

- **Sharp grey bob** – regardless of whether this remotely suits the shape of her face. Hampstead Lady thinks 'like Louise Brooks'. Hampstead Lady is wrong.

- **Big, heavy spectacles** – the £400 version of those old NHS ones. Hampstead Lady thinks 'playful yet serious, with an ironic nod to Aneurin Bevan'. Mmm.

- **Vast, shapeless, genderless, sexless Japanese or Scandinavian clothes** – often with artful folds. Hampstead Lady thinks 'these clothes are like art'. Maybe, Hampstead Lady, maybe. But you look like you're a size 26 and have never had sex – even though both of these statements are untrue, probably.

- **Birkenstocks or men's brogues.** Maybe all their feet are horribly sore, I don't know (and see page 15 for feet things). But again, the deliberate un-gendering can appear strange to the onlooker. Nothing wrong with a pair of Birkies, of course, and I happen to love brogues. But worn beneath the giganto pleated number, you just look like you're walking around permanently thinking, 'Ugh, there'll be no bedroom unpleasantness around here.' It's hostile.

- **No make-up, or 'no-make-up' make-up** – like it's a badge of honour. Would you like a medal? (No make-up, or 'no-make-up' make-up, just because you don't fancy it is fine. But there's a variant on it that says, 'I'm no flibber-tigibbet.' It's OK – we got that already, from the clothes.)

- **Sometimes Hampstead Lady will wear a slash of red lipstick** – in the manner of a beautiful French ingénue. The slash of red lipstick can look amazing or quite kabuki,[1] but remember that red makes your teeth look yellow. Or more yellow, in this case. They need to be super-white to start with (see page 21).

- **Geometric accessories** – to go with the geometric, 'sculptural' clothing: angular bracelets, spiky necklaces. I mean, they're fine. They're just totally Hampstead Lady.

To be fair, Hampstead Lady sometimes – though not always – dresses the way that she does because she feels herself to be unusually large. She very rarely is. The problem generally with loose, baggy clothes is that you completely lose track of what size you really are. You're so used to your vast silhouette that you forget you're actually a size 12.

But even if you're not, given that you can now easily buy attractive clothing in up to a size 24 cheaply and at the click of a mouse – see ASOS Curve, for instance – there is no excuse to hide under tents unless you're going camping. The impulse to tent up will exist, of course, because tents used to be all that was available,

[1] The late Diana Vreeland, of both *Vogue* and *Harper's Bazaar*, admired the kabuki look so much that she rouged her earlobes every day.

and all that was comfy. But that's no longer true. Also, as a size 16 myself, I say this to you from the heart: there is nothing, *nothing* that makes you look fatter than loose, shapeless garments. If I want to look beached, I stick on a smock. If I want to look nice, I belt it. If I want to look and feel comfortable, I wear something relatively loose-fitting but, crucially, in my size – not too big.

The other terrible mistake is when you're a different size on top than you are on the bottom, and you wear one huge item because it's all that fits. It *is* possible to buy clothes that fit if you have big bosoms; I do it all the time. Saint Bustier's website[2] is a good starting point. And, needless to say, decent underwear, for which you have been measured properly, is essential here. Now's not the time to slouch around in old bras that are anything other than exactly the right size and in pristine nick, i.e. maximally supportive.

Anyway – COLOUR, as I was saying before I got massively sidetracked. I won't pretend it's entirely without peril if you're colour shy, or even colourphobic. Misunderstanding colour, or discovering it and suddenly loving it too much, is what can lead to Whacky – and, as we have seen, Whacky is to be avoided at all costs. Ease yourself in gently:

[2] saintbustier.com

* **If you can do pale pink,** you can ramp it up gradually, until you end up with red (never top to toe, otherwise people start singing Chris de Burgh at you).

* **If you can do navy,** and there isn't a person alive who can't, then you can lighten the shade and wear teal (lovely on brunettes), petrol blue and turquoise.

And so on. Colours have a marvellous effect on morale. Plus, if you're one of those people who feel 'invisible' in the sartorial equivalent of magnolia, you will feel more present by wearing actual shades.

INVISIBILITY

Here's what I think: that 'feeling invisible' is an old chestnut. You're not invisible to your tribe. And if you are, you've just made yourself that way, with your uncertainty. If you think you're invisible because groups of boys don't catcall after you in the street any more – well, be grateful. Who wants people young enough to be their children to catcall after them? It's creepy, and it's not a sane reason for feeling invisible. So waiters don't flirt with you. So what? Both of my sons have been waiters; I really wouldn't want them to

62

have flirted with my friends. I mean, *grue-some*. Most people are brought up to respect their elders, and that's a good thing.

No, you can only really say you're invisible if you never catch the eye or attention of someone your own age, or from your own generation. Which I bet you do. Therefore, everything is as it should be. When you were twenty, you didn't want to be ogled by ten-year-olds or by thirty-year-olds. You wanted the people in your age group to look at you and pay attention to you. They still do. Having said all of that, terrible hair and clothes *can* certainly cause you to fade into the background somewhat.

If you don't like it out there, in the background, read on.

MUTTON

This is, I think, what a lot of women are terrified of, with good reason. It's why they go into a department store, feel panicked, think, 'There's too much stuff! I don't know where to start! I don't understand fashion any more!' and end up buying the blandest, most inoffensive thing they can find. Yes, it's boring, but at least it's not – shudder – 'age-inappropriate'. It's not mutton, i.e. it is not the Great Satan, the Hornèd One, in clothes form.

What is Mutton?

Here's what I have discovered about mutton: it's all in the way you wear it. You can wear ONE muttonish thing, and maybe even two, but the rest of you has to be relatively sober. The list of things that are muttonish is actually quite small, when you examine it:

* **Very short skirts,** even if your legs are amazing. M-U-T-T-O-N.

* **But not, oddly, short shorts** (at the beach – not in the office. If you're going to wear short shorts to the office, don't forget to stick on a little woolly tail).

* **Dressing like you're at a music festival,** unless you are at a music festival.

* **Dressing like you're married to a rock star,** unless you are married to a rock star.

* **Over-cleavage.** 'Hey, everyone! I've got tits! Two of 'em! Two whole human tits, right here, in my top. Yep. How about that, huh?' Excusable in an adolescent, problematic in yer actual nan.

* **Spindly heels** – block heels are fine. Obviously, this depends on fashion, but thin spike heels make an awful lot of outfits look

either questionable or try-hard, at our age. Also, that stiletto shape calls to mind the 1950s, when you were born. And if your feet hurt – and lots of people's do in this age bracket – then you're tottering about on spindly heels with a pained expression ('poo face', as it's known in my house), and that's a double fault.

And that's kind of it. And even then: very short skirts with the densest opaque or woolly tights can work; taking only some elements of music festival or rock-star wife can work beautifully; over-cleavage isn't the end of the world if your cleavage is magnificent. And things that are traditionally mutton – leather, say – all depend on how you wear them. A leather dress from Camden Market that laces saucily (groo) up the sides: maybe not. But leather leggings with a white shirt, an oversized navy cashmere jumper and flat shoes: why not? (I really love leather leggings because they're incredibly comfortable and also because they *wipe clean* if you spill stuff on them. So practical! The makers of leather garments are missing a marketing trick. There's quite a good argument to be made for new mothers and very old people wearing leather clothing at all times, like badasses.)

Ditto denim: maybe not the batty riders and the cheesecloth shirt tied around the midriff. But let no one impugn the noble pair of jeans, or the denim jacket. (Denim looks especially brilliant with grey hair.[3])

Pare it Down

If you're paranoid about mutton, remember the mantra that less is more. If the garment you're wearing feels questionable to you on the mutton front, tone everything else you're wearing down, and 99.9 per cent of the time, you'll be fine. If I wear 'younger' clothes – which, to be honest, I do every day – then I wear very little make-up, or a made-up version of 'very little make-up'. If I wear something 'grown-up', like a smart structured dress, I whack on the eyeshadow and the old lippy. Though having said that, it can work both ways: the smart structured dress looks more youthful without the face full of slap. As I was saying, less is more.

Case in point, mutton-wise: leopard print. It's taken me about five years to come around to my friend Sali's assertion that 'leopard is a neutral': to me, leopard over the age of thirty was more 'working down the docks, charging extra for anal'. And sure, you can make leopard work like that very easily – if it's mangy, if it's clearly vintage and the rest of your look isn't, if you've had it since

[3] Do you know why we get grey hair? Because we run out of pigment cells, the cells that make hair colour. Stem cells help the pigment cells out, but then they too get used up, and that is that.

you were sixteen and discovered shopping at Oxfam, back in the days when it was still called 'second-hand'. If it's pert and newish, on the other hand, it looks fabulous. The thing to remember about leopard is that it roars all by itself – it's not a lily that needs any gilding. Personally, I love a leopard-and-red-lipstick combo, with maybe flicky eyeliner and a pair of stilettoes, but this is steering dangerously (you might say pleasingly) close to mutton-stroke-parody territory. Of course you can do knowing, ironic mutton – but not unless you're 100 per cent sure that you can carry it off, looking like you're in on the joke. I mean, dressing like Rizzo from *Grease* occasionally: what's not to like?

And so it turns out that there's no such thing as mutton, really. There is, obviously – it exists, and we all recognize it. But there's no actual individual garment that forces mutton upon you, with the possible exception of the miniskirt. Mutton comes when *too many* garments and accessories (make-up included) spoil the broth. So we should be vigilant, but we should not be fearful.

Mother of the Bride

At the other end of the mutton axis, we have Mother Of The Bride – another look that it is tragically easy for the confused older woman to fall into. It's an abyss, MOTB, and it's quite hard to climb out again once you've fallen in. When I say MOTB, I don't mean it literally. I mean the daily application of this particular look – 'smart casual', you might say, with a heavy reliance on 'outfits'. Matchy-matchy. Smart, but in the wrong (ageing) way. Easy to put together, and a favourite of women in positions of power or authority. But ask yourself: do you really want to spend your Prime walking around looking like you're about to chair a board meeting? It's safe, that kind of clothing, and it's a bit like armour – no wonder Hillary Clinton's fans call themselves the Sisterhood of the Travelling Pantsuits.

Tangentially, I really hate 'power dressing', a) because it's so eighties and b) because to me it smacks of a time when powerful women were such a rarity that they had to dress like men to be taken seriously. I like to think we're past those days – I mean, we're still no closer to sodding equal pay, and the struggle very much continues, but the idea that pantsuits (hahaha) are the way to get things done sounds very retrograde to me. It would be so much cooler if a powerful woman turned up in a tea dress and a pair of Hasbeens,[4] instead of trussed up in a stupid old suit – or its more feminine equivalent, the stupid old shift dress and matching jacket.

Anyway: MOTB. Here's how not to do it:

* **Don't always buy things that 'go'.** Just because that particular skirt is next to that

[4] swedishhasbeens.com

particular top doesn't mean you have to buy the entire display. You might have the perfect top at home, or the perfect top might be hanging at the other end of the store.

* **Buy the item you love because you absolutely love it,** and work from there. Don't buy it because it 'matches' a particular pair of shoes or a particular jacket. Shopping this way is boring – and you end up looking boring, too.

* **MOTB is very good at hiding the figure** – it loves blocky shapes. As I will never tire of saying, it doesn't matter if your waist is enormous – show you have one. Clothing that is marketed as 'flattering' is often clothing that just hides you. As we have seen, hiding is not good for either morale or aesthetics.

* **Beware clothes that 'skim' over 'the bad bits'.** I mean, yeah – if you look pregnant even though you're not, then you probably want something that's loose over the stomach. But it doesn't mean it has to be loose over the tits as well.

* **Never, ever, ever buy anything 'waterfall'.** It's the one sure-fire way of saying, 'Inside, I'm ninety-two and waiting for death.'

* **MOTB colours:** eau de nil, beige, pale blue. Beige. Beige. Beige. Tip: MOTB colours are always very slightly 'off'. A blue that's a weird blue, a pink that's too purply, a yellow that's not found in nature. If you find yourself thinking, 'Heh, funny colour,' put it back on the rail.

Feet First . . . and Last

One last thing: shoes. If you want to make yourself look instantly older and in need of medical attention, wear shoes that don't fit. Swollen-looking feet crammed into shoes that are too tight is just the pits of looks. It immediately calls to mind very old ladies, possibly immobilized. Always, *always* wear shoes that fit and that are comfortable. If they don't fit, don't buy them: the end.

I'm not going to go into my foot rant again, but really – your feet are keeping you upright. Don't fuck with 'em. They want trainers? Give 'em trainers. (Trainers look cool with everything and are comfy as hell.) Wear trainers, I say. Personalize yours online at NIKEiD.[5]

[5] nike.com/gb/en_gb/c/nikeid

CHAPTER 3

SEX AND RELATIONSHIPS

*With partners; dating and sex;
and how to get divorced*

One of the things that I like best of all about being older is that I never – literally, never – give myself a hard time over the subject of relationships. This makes a monumental change from the whole of my teens, twenties and thirties and feels like the most extraordinary liberation. Thinking about it, this has come about partly through experience and partly (mostly) with the dawning realization that everything is possible, that you don't have to wedge yourself into some neat little slot/round hole if you don't feel like it, that the universe/family unit won't collapse if you don't, that all sorts of people live in all sorts of ways – in short, that whatever works for you is the right choice, provided you're not some kind of monster that gets off on hurting other people.

What works for you may very well be the neat, nuclear family option. But it may be something else altogether. It may be the person you've been with since you were sixteen, and it may be the one you met last week. The point is, everything is fine. And if it doesn't feel fine – well, you're free to do something about it. There it is in stark black and white: you're in your Prime, and you're an adult; you can see things clearly, you can fix things, and you can even walk away from them if you want to.

Having said that, there is nitty-gritty to be examined here.

MARRIED SEX

Let's start with married sex – I say 'married' for ease but I mean any kind of long-term, cohabiting sex, a decade or two in. This, it seems to me, is breakdownable into two distinct categories: Not Much Sex (Happy) and Not Much Sex (Sad). Category three – Heaps Of Sex, Thumbs Up – doesn't really need any help. I'm talking here about long-term relationships in and past middle age, just to be clear, and so I am making all sorts of assumptions: chiefly, the assumption that the knackered-all-the-time, sleep-is-better-than-sex, small-children years are behind you. You emerge from that period blinking into the light, you catch up on about ten years' worth of sleep, and – well, now what? Pants down, that's what. In theory.

Not Much Sex (Happy)

Some couples never really recover from the not-much-sex years (which in some acute cases are the no-sex years, or sex-under-duress years – either way, not much fun). They have fallen into certain patterns and rhythms, and while sex features occasionally, it certainly isn't the central point of the relationship. Talking to friends, I note that people inside this kind of relationship – which I admire: it's so Radio 4ish and crosswordy and *cosy* – occasionally worry about the fact that everybody is having, or claiming to have, more sex than they are, that they 'should' have sex more often, that their partner may silently be incredibly sexually frustrated and end up having affairs, and so on.

Ask yourself: who cares about how much sex other people are or aren't having, and how their tally compares with yours? (Plus, we're talking here about people so busy having loads of sizzlin' sex that they have the time to answer telephone surveys on their bedtime habits. It's not un-suspect, is it?) They're not you; they're not your partner; they're not in your specific, unique relationship. It is simply too silly to worry about this. If things are ticking along companionably and your appetites seem more or less aligned, hurrah. Count your blessings: people would kill for what you have. You have Not Much Sex (Happy), and that's just dandy.

Of course there exist some utter snakes in the grass, capable of being bigamists or trigamists on the sly, without anyone ever finding out, but they're pretty thin on the ground. When it comes to the possibility of **infidelity**, you can usually see (if you're not too busy burying your head firmly in the sand), or rather *sense* it coming.

Infidelity is primarily to do with sex and desire, obviously, but it also has to do with elements of vanity – not just the person's desire to have sex with somebody else, but their own need for sexual validation and their need to feel desired and wanted. That's a massive generalization, of course – some people just really like shagging and aren't overly troubled by conscience (I'll get to those in a minute) – but I think it broadly holds true. It is certainly true that middle-aged men are prone to crises of confidence, and may roam outside the nest to validate their virility – or to make sure they are, in fact, still virile and sexually appealing. So then you realize that there is a kind of awful *neediness* to some adulterers, which is tremendously unattractive and worthy of pity (young women who specialize in having affairs with older men understand this perfectly and use the neediness to their own advantage). It is perhaps more worthy of pity than of rage.

I'm not going to mount a defence of adultery, but I genuinely wonder how much it matters to our hypothetical long-married couple (everything I am saying here applies to one-off adultery, not repeated instances of sexual incontinence). If you're twenty-five and your boyfriend shags somebody else – well, it's the end of days, obviously, because he's supposed to be your boyfriend. If he wants to shag other people, then what on earth is he doing with you? You're young and narcissistic and in the first flush of desire, and the solution seems glaringly simple: you break up with him, so he can go and shag this person whom he clearly wants more than he wants you.

When you have been married twenty years, and you're fifty, and you have children, and a house, and joint financial arrangements, you might pause and ask yourself whether chucking him out really is the best solution. Of course, the betrayal is much greater than that of some silly boyfriend when you were eighteen, and the pain inflicted is much more acute. But is it really worth effectively binning the life you have made together over two decades? As we have seen, the adulterer is partly to be pitied: he wants proof that he's still hot, which is sad, however you cut it, and maybe a teeny bit deserving of sympathy. (Wouldn't you like proof that you're still hot? How are you going to get it if yours is basically a sexless union?) He goes off, he sleeps with somebody else, you either discover his infidelity or, tormented by his conscience, he fesses up. I'm not convinced that behaving as though you're in a soap opera – screaming yourself hoarse and showing him the door – is necessarily the sensible solution here. Scream yourself hoarse, by all means, but then sit down and think. Impulsiveness is not a friend here.

Yes, lots of affairs are terminal – too many, if you ask me, because we've been conditioned to think they're the end of everything, rather than crappy but manageable, like a broken limb or small head wound. And obviously someone who ran around shagging everything that moved, again and again, just because he could, well, really – that's showing neither love nor respect for you, and he should go and do that from a flat of his own, wearing the Cone Of Shame, rather than from the marital home. But I also think that the odd blip – the oner or twoer (max) over a period of decades – is, if not quite excusable, then at least humanly understandable.

Sometimes a stupid ill-advised shag really is just a stupid ill-advised shag. I remember years ago remonstrating with an old friend, who'd got drunk on a trip and hopped into bed with someone or other, and of course his wife found out and evicted him on the spot. 'What a sodding waste,' he said. 'It's a complete disaster. Plus the sex was terrible. I could barely get a semi.'

What I am actually doing is beating around the bush and trying to think of a more palatable way of saying, 'Affairs: so what?' This isn't quite what I think – if it happened to me we'd be talking murderous rampage, but then I have a regrettably short temper. In the cold light of day, though, I think that, like many women, I might be inclined – through the benefits of being older, wiser and less judgemental – to think, 'Stupid arse. I am really, really pissed off and upset, but I think we can probably work it through.' Maybe.

Extra-Marital Sex

Now, a word about extra-marital shagging more generally. I know everybody thinks their partner is a paragon of virtue who would never dream of breaking his sacred wedding vows, but I'm also quite old and quite observant. It doesn't matter how much sex the man has at home (and most men in this category feel they don't have enough, even if you're constantly shagging and can barely walk). My conclusion is this: if there was a 100 per cent guarantee of not being found out – of no comeback and no consequences – most men would shag other people if they could. Where alcohol is involved, many men *do* shag other people. The man, a bit pissed, who is offered no-strings sex with someone he fancies, knowing nobody will ever find out, and who turns it down, is a rare beast. He is a hen with teeth and a winged pig. It's not very nice, but there we are. And of course it takes two: a sizeable minority of women feel exactly the same way. It's not hurting anybody; it passes the time; it's jollier than sitting in your hotel room watching the news in a foreign language, and so on. It's so irrelevant to normal, everyday life that after a while it barely registers. And yes, of course people feel bad: infidelity never makes anybody feel terrific. The unfortunate thing is that they feel really bad the first time, less bad the second, a bit bad the third, and not bad at all the fourth. By adventure number fifteen, feeling bad doesn't come into it.

* **Only you can tell whether you are happy being part of a union where adultery occurs,** whether it's once or serially. If it's any comfort, neither occasional adultery nor serial shagging *usually* results in people announcing that they want to leave and be with the hook-up; that doesn't of course mean that it *never* happens. All of those clichés and tropes – 'It meant nothing', 'It's you I love', and so forth – are often absolutely true. But sometimes they're not.

* **For every world-weary thing that I've said, never underestimate love.** Love is amazing, and there exists a particular kind of love that really can cause you to say, 'Sorry, handsome tempter/beautiful temptress, standing there in your powerfully appealing underwear, but I must leave now, before anything happens, for I love another.'

LATE-ONSET DIVORCE

This is when you have been with your husband since forever, rubbing along companionably enough, fond of each other and broadly happy. And then retirement comes, and suddenly you're together all day long. Recent figures show that the divorce rate spikes around retirement age: the number of 'silver splitters' has risen by three-quarters in the past twenty years, according to an Office for National Statistics report from 2013.[1] One of the reasons is that people do that awful thing of waiting until the children are grown up before filing for the divorce they've wanted for years. (Bad, bad idea. One life! One shot! Plus, imagine those grown-up children's sense of betrayal when it turns out their entire childhood was based on a lie.) Another reason is that some people wait until retirement to have their mid-life crises. The third reason is that sometimes two people who are used to living two lives – one with each other, one at work – find themselves with just the domestic one, almost overnight, and it's not an adjustment everybody is automatically happy with, or indeed capable of making. Not only have they lost the thing that partially defines them – their occupation – but they are now at home all day. And not only that, but at home all day *with each other*.

If your marriage worked *because* it involved a degree of outside (work) life and physical separation, it may totter and

---

[1] There were 15,300 people of either gender over the age of sixty getting divorced in 2011, the most recent year for which official figures are available. By contrast in 1991, there were just 8,700.

wobble now that both of you are in the house together – all day, every day – with nothing to demarcate the weekdays from the weekends. And what is there to talk about at dinner, when neither of you brings news of the outside world, of office life, of an amusing or interesting thing you saw on your way to lunch? Now there is only the inside world, and you're both stuck in it.

How can you ignore the things about your partner that irritate you, now that his habits, like him, are constantly present? It's one thing to be annoyed by them twice a day – quite another to be annoyed twice an hour.

Nevertheless, I think that a lot of late-onset divorces are on the hasty side. If you've longed for a separation for the past twenty years, fine. If not, then all of the questions above have sensible answers. Of course it can feel suffocating and claustrophobic to spend every minute of your waking life – your sleeping one too, actually – with the same person, especially when you're not used to it, especially when, in your head, the relationship has only survived for as long as it has precisely because you've both done your own things. Think about the following, though, before you do anything too drastic:

- **You would feel claustrophobic and suffocated with anyone,** in these 24/7 circumstances. You'd feel it even more acutely with a new partner, because the person wouldn't be your spouse, who at least knows you like the back of his hand.

- **If you're feeling claustrophobic, the chances are that he is, too.** Physical space is often a solution here – it's why men have always loved their sheds and allotments. If you can find different spaces to be in during various parts of the day, you might both feel much happier.

- **Often a problem arises because the woman has girlfriends and hobbies,** and the man doesn't (men often have two close friends, if that, whereas women often have dozens). The woman feels bad when she goes off and does things with her friends, leaving the man to mooch about listlessly on his own. But she shouldn't feel bad. Men love mooching listlessly, though of course this can sometimes be a euphemism for 'being left alone to look at porn' (good luck to them. I am pro-porn, unless the porn is illegal).

- **Taking up sports or other activities** is a sort of retirement cliché – all that golf – but, like most clichés, it has its roots in truth. There is nothing wrong – on the contrary – with finding a new hobby and devoting a goodly amount of time to it. You're out having fun, you're meeting new people, and you may even see the burgeoning of a latent talent, if the hobby is something like painting or creative writing. Don't for heaven's sake take these up together – find separate things to do. The couple that plays apart stays together, I always say – or I would if it didn't sound slightly dodgy and sexual, which is not what I mean here at all.

Sometimes late-onset divorce happens because one or other partner thinks, 'He [or she] isn't like I thought they were at all. They've changed! All these years, and I never really noticed until now.' Well, yes – of course they've changed. They're living creatures, not ammonites. Having all of that leisure time to notice the changes may seem a bit alarming or bizarre, but don't see it that way. Think, 'How fascinating – the person I know and love, but with new bits.' The point is, you might absolutely *love* the new bits. Don't knock them till you've tried them.

Don't run about going, 'Woah, change, I don't like change, *woah.*' Actually, you do like change. We all do. Change is what saves us from dying of boredom (and see page 271 for change in the context of moving house or downsizing).

Keeping Your Relationship Alive

At the opposite end of the cosy, crosswords-and-Radio-4 version of the long old marriage, you have the people who do everything in their power to keep things fresh – both for their own sanity and as a means of attempting to swerve round the complicated scenarios described above. And it's such an interesting question, that notion of not letting yourself or anything else 'go'. It's super old-fashioned: it's a woman's mother in 1952 making a cat's-bum mouth and saying, 'You've let yourself go. Be careful or you'll lose him.' I mean, it's ludicrous, in this day and age. Right? *Right?*

Well, yes. Mostly. It's mostly ludicrous, but it's also a little bit true.

Here is the thing that I sometimes want to shout in people's faces, because they really don't get it: your partner isn't necessarily cool with you putting on three stone overnight, at the same time as deciding that hair removal is a pointless faff (especially the tache), at the same time as giving all your clothes to the charity shop because you've decided you're happiest in a giant she-tent, at the same time as deciding the best underwear for you is the giant granny pant, extra-long and extra-large (with a strong ol' reinforced gusset), to the exclusion of all others. Yes, you are allowed to make all of those choices. You are allowed to be anything at all that you like – to look how you like and wear what you like and act how you like. What you are not allowed to do is be so spoilt and entitled that you think that these changes and actions will have no consequences – or, worse, to think that the consequences are an outrage.

It's annoying me that this feels like a controversial, maybe even un-feminist thing to write. But come on. Come *on*. Everything cuts both ways: would you be cool if your partner suddenly developed one of those paunches that made him look like a heavily pregnant egg, stopped cutting his toenails, grew a massive mujahidin beard and sat around farting like a horse, saying, 'You know what, I really like myself this way. I feel so authentic and great'? I mean, you know. You could be forgiven for feeling discomfited, or indeed extremely put out.

Marriage is a contract, and both people sign it. This doesn't mean that it is your 'duty' not to get fat, or your husband's 'duty' not to have a little paunch, and of course nobody's so shallow that they stop loving the person over a question of chubby arms or the odd stone here or there. But there are limits, and it behoves us to bear them in mind. Again, we come across the difference between love and desire. Ideally, you want both. And so, ideally, you want to bear in mind physical maintenance of some sort.

My main piece of advice, though, is this: keep your marriage happy by not asking too much of it. People are imperfect. Life is imperfect. So what? It's not worth freaking out over dishwasher loading or the route you took to Norfolk. Little daily annoyances are an irrelevance, even if they do build up over the years. The small stuff is so very, very small, and love is so big.

WEIRD, INAPPROPRIATE CRUSHES

These are so strange. Everyone gets them at some point, often near the end of the first stage of marriage, when the exciting shine has rubbed off a bit (they can also occur in the middle of an arduous meno-pause). Crushes usually happen at work. The colleague who you like but have never looked at twice in that way suddenly becomes extraordinarily, magnetically attractive. You find yourself giggling when he makes jokes, possibly in a weird new girlish tone you never knew you had. If you had a fan, you'd tap him saucily with it, exclaiming, 'Fie, sirrah!' Your behaviour around him becomes compulsively, almost obsessively flirtatious. If he flirts back – which is to be hoped, otherwise this one-sided situation is just really (extra) embarrassing – you start wondering what it would be like to snog him. Sometimes you *do* snog him. Some people go abso-lutely doolally and decide that they are, in fact, in love with the weird, inappropriate crush. But in fact they never are. They're just having a turn.

If you find yourself in this situation – and it could be a colleague but it could also be, I don't know, the Ocado man or the pool guy (do people have pool guys in the UK? Hilarious notion) – my advice is to flirt all you like but NOT snog the Ocado man, or whoever, because actually he is not your one true love, he does not see right into your very soul and he doesn't really have the soul of a poet or trouba-dour. You are merely either a) menopausal or b) proving to yourself that other men still find you attractive.

And then, one day, the crush is gone – just like that – and the colleague is just a colleague/Ocado man/pool guy again.

Not Much Sex (Sad)

This is quite a bleak scenario. It is, of course, possible to exist with your sexuality completely in abeyance, and to do so for considerable periods of time. But it's not good because a) when it does rear up, beware (this is often how people get into really complicated and loony situations – less an injudicious affair, more suddenly exploding and bumming ten rent boys while dragging on a crack pipe) and b) wanting to have sex, and not having it despite being in a relationship, is a sorry state of affairs. How sorry depends to an extent on your history of sexual activity – if you are a person who's never had much sex, it may be fine (in which case you're Not Much Sex (Happy) and can stop reading this bit).

Oh, Not Much Sex (Sad) really *is* sad. I wish I could think of an ingenious solution. I guess it's a question of whether the Not Much Sex is simply a question of mismatched libidos, in which case it's probably OK to carry on as you are (and, presumably, have been for a long time) – on the basis that, if nothing else, at least you're used to it. If it's a question of feeling horribly undesired, though, then it's just grim and demoralizing. I don't know that a person can reasonably be expected to hack that amount of rejection. Your self-esteem would just wither away to nothing, and the effects of this would seep into every aspect of your life – people who are undesired and feel unwanted tend to get infected with an all-purpose sourness. I say, get out. Life is short, and getting shorter every day. But it's never too short to make a new start.

HOW TO GET DIVORCED

I really know my onions here. The father of my sons is my first husband, a dear friend and the godfather of my daughter. The father of my daughter – my former partner – lives one street away and is also a dear friend. I do not believe in hideous divorces or separations, possibly because as a child and young adult I had my fair share of living with the aftermath of hideous divorces. It is not something I would wish on my worst enemy, let alone on a child. The crossfire is horrendous. Avoid placing yourself, and people you love, in it. Here are some tips.

(Disclaimer: the below applies to 'normal' divorces – although one of the problems is that people always feel their own divorces to be exceptional (they aren't). What I mean is, these recommendations don't apply in quite the same way if your ex (let's say it's an ex-husband) is bad, or really mad, and you have the kind of divorce that requires you to be taken to a safe house.)

- **If you're young, or youngish, and don't have kids:** it's not that big a deal. Sorry, it just isn't. It's really sad and you will feel terrible for a while, but you will recover, and you will (yes, you will) find love again. You were with somebody, and now you're not, and you have a piece of paper saying so. There we are. It happens to thousands of people, every day. Let's all move on, like the capable adults we know how to be.

- **If you do have children:** remember the person you are divorcing is their dad and they will never have another. It would be well to bear in mind that you chose to be with this man of your own free will. There were things about him that were simply fantastic, things you loved so much that you wanted to marry him, make a family with him and stay with him until the end of your life.

- **Yes, it's sad that you fell out of love with each other.** On the other hand, neither of you had a sudden personality transplant. The qualities that drew you to that person still exist: the person is still clever, or funny, or kind or insightful. They still love French novels, the smell of wet pavements ('petrichor', it's called – nice word) and macaroni cheese. The awful, sad things that neither of you anticipated and that derailed your rela-tionship can now be left behind. They're over: you're divorced. You don't have to deal with them any more.

- **After a suitable period of mourning the death of your love for each other** – and of feeling sorry for yourself because WHO WILL HAVE YOU NOW? and YOU WILL DIE ALONE – gather your wits and celebrate the part of the relationship that needs to stay alive and needs to keep functioning: the parenting part.

- **The alive part is bigger than the dead part.** As co-parents, the person will always be in your life. I repeat: you loved this person. You loved them enough to have children with them.

- **They have not stopped being the person you loved.** You just don't love them *in that way* any more. And that is fine. It doesn't mean you can't ever chat about French novels while eating macaroni cheese, on wet pavements.

- **Of course you feel anger, disappointment, rancour, guilt/betrayal, deep sorrow** – all of the things. But these all pass. They pass a lot faster if you don't sit in the dark obsessing about them.

Obsessing over something that you cannot change is a form of self-harm. Give yourself a present: value yourself enough to go and do something else instead.

- **I'm not saying that separation is easy.** When my daughter's father and I split up, I cried hysterically for days (actually, I cried so ridiculously and incontinently that I astonished myself. At one point I took a picture of the amazing crying, which struck me as an almost medical phenomenon[2]). And then I stopped crying and, weirdly, after a while everything was fine. It was like being hungry and needing to eat: I needed to cry hysterically, and once I'd finished crying, off I trotted, really quite cheerfully, on my two little hooves, tossin' my mane.

- **Never, ever bad-mouth your former partner to anybody**. First, it makes you sound sour, obsessive and mad. Second, it's incredibly awkward for the somebody (or somebodies) who is (or are) probably a mutual friend and who has

---

[2] This sounds awful. But I'm a journalist. It was sad, but also *interesting*.

no desire, quite rightly, to be forced into taking sides. Third, if you force them into the uncomfortable position of having to choose, be aware that it may not be the ranting, irate, destructive you that they choose to side with.

- **Most crucially, never, ever bad-mouth your former partner to your children.** Doing this is the absolute pits, and it holds true whether your children are five or twenty-five or fifty. There is no person on earth – not one – who is happy that his or her mother trashed their dad (or vice versa) throughout their childhood, or indeed adulthood. Anger infects everything. You're perfectly allowed to be angry, but go and bellow at the sky from the top of a hill. Don't bellow near your children, or – even worse – weep near them. Weeping near your children, and saying horrendous things like 'Daddy's left us' is disgusting and unpardonable.

- **Sly digs at your ex are even worse than anger and weeping.** Saying, 'He's just not the person I thought he was,' while shaking your head – the whole 'more in sorrow than in anger' thing – is awful. At least with shouting

94

and crying, you're presenting yourself as someone who is emoting wildly. Sly digs in a reasonable voice are even more confusing, because they make you sound plausible.

- **Never force said children to take sides.** If I was Queen of the World, I'd have those parents done for emotional harm.

- **Be flexible.** There needs to be some give and take in the new arrangements. So he's a bit late. Really – so what? Yanking the door open while tapping your watch is a total waste of time. It just generates more anger/resentment/unreasonableness. If your children are young and he said he'd have them for the weekend and cancels at the last minute, ask yourself: is it really that big a deal? You live with the children anyway. Also, when you're whisked off for a sexy minibreak with your new boyfriend in a year's time (because, actually, you won't die alone, being eaten by cats), you can legitimately call on your ex to step in and help. This is harder to do if your relationship with him consists of you being an utter nightmare.

- **When it comes to visits and access, always give as much notice as you can:** of holidays, weekends away, work trips and times you won't be around. For absolutely failsafe security, and so that nobody can say, 'But you didn't tell me,' you could do a lot worse than set up an online calendar that you can both access and fill in. Also, if you suddenly find you're going to go somewhere, always email the other parent immediately to say, 'I'm away for these dates and I've put them in the joint diary.' It takes two seconds. Visits that don't happen and missed dates are annoying for everybody, and upsetting for children. That doesn't mean you won't encounter the occasional cock-up through nobody's particular fault. Take it in your stride.

- **Never be overly polite, or falsely grand, about financial arrangements.** This is crucial: you may long to tell him to stick his stupid alimony up his jacksie, but there is no point in cutting off your nose to spite your face. Get arrangements in place early and matter-of-factly. Don't say, 'We'll manage,' and feel all pointlessly noble. His children, his shared expenses: the end.

- **Let it go. Let it goooooo.** All the bad/ mad/annoying things are in the past. The only person you're harming by harping on about them is you – and, if you do it within their earshot, your children. To be brutal: nobody else cares that much. They're sad for you – and sympathetic, of course – but they have their own lives to be getting on with. So it's just you, festering there. You could be painting your toenails and drinking gin instead.

- **Remember, there was more good than bad** – unless you're really exceptionally unfortunate and the union was a vile disaster from the moment the wedding guests went home. Basically, you've banked a lot of good things, good times, good memories – days and weeks and months and years unwasted and spent happily and well. That, in itself, is an amazing, towering achievement. Look to your laurels.

- **If you do all of these things, your life, and the lives of your loved ones, becomes dramatically happier.** Middle age and beyond is a time of shedding all the crap and forging ahead. It is very much not the time to sit brooding

97

furiously over what might have been. Leave that to teenagers, and be glad you're old enough not to be a twat.

PS: If you *have* been a twat, and can't even pronounce your ex's name without doing weird twitching and having a hissy fit, well, this stuff is rather like dieting or taking up exercise – no time like the present. Make a start. Don't be one of those terrible, terrible people who ruin their children's weddings by being unable to be in the same room as each other.

WHAT IF YOU'RE SINGLE?

First off: being single can be marvellous. It's not an illness or an affliction. It can feel like gulping down fresh air after a period spent in a window-less room. I am very much not knocking it: when I've been single, I've really liked it. Loved it, actually, because I really love the feeling that anything can happen and that some fantastic adventure may be just around the corner.

What if it isn't, though? What if nothing happens, and if you really want something to happen? Are you going to languish at the dinner tables of your married friends, waiting for them to toss you a crumb in the shape of the one 'eligible' single man they manage to dredge up from somewhere (the very depths, usually)? We all did that in our twenties or thirties, and it wasn't especially rewarding then: do we really have to go through the whole charade again in middle age? If your answer to that is no, then you have to take matters into your own capable hands.

I'm going to say something annoying again here, which is that I don't understand why people who don't want to be single *are* single. I don't get it. It's difficult to find the love of your life, yes – it's needle-in-a-haystack, once-in-a-lifetime stuff (or twice, or thrice, depending on your levels of optimism). But it's really not at all difficult to find someone to go on a date with, or to sleep with. It's just not.

HOW TO DATE

1. **What is it you want?** Obvious sort of question, but worth answering it realistically. Do you want a fun evening out, or are you holding out for something more serious? See, I think the *only* possible answer here is 'a fun evening out'. You need to start with the basics. People trip themselves up with this stuff by stubbornly going 'I want a life partner' or 'I want Rhett Butler in *Gone with the Wind*' or 'I want somebody over six foot, with blue eyes, who's a doctor' or 'I want someone to go on holiday with next month' or 'I want somebody unbelievably hot, to make my ex jealous' (worst reason. Are you twelve?). The people who enter the dating world with these silly demands are the ones who are still wringing their hands three years later, baffled by their singledom. You're not writing a shopping list. That height thing: you're just being weird. Ditto eye colour. Ditto job.

2. **So you want a fun evening out (or a fun lunch).** If this whole dating business makes you anxious, do it at lunchtime. Elevenses, even. Teatime. It doesn't have to feel like a big

momentous thing, which dinner always does, especially in winter when it's dark, which reminds everyone unhelpfully of going to bed.

3. **Do you know anyone single you'd like to have a fun evening out with?** Not at first glance, or you'd be having the FEO instead of reading this. But cast your net wide. That attractive man who flirted with you three years ago, when you were with somebody else – what about him? Thingy from university, who's popped up on Facebook and whose jokes make you laugh? The man who lives nearby, who you sometimes bump into in Tesco Express, by the lettuces? I mean, everyone's fair game. They'd also rather be having a FEO than sitting at home flicking through the channels, is the thing to bear in mind. It's not going to kill you to ask them. I once had a FEO with a man I met when I was standing in the middle of the pavement, texting.

4. **Too shy for that sort of thing?** Fair enough (though a shame, in my opinion, because by and large the best dates, like the best parties, aren't the ones that are carefully engineered). It's perfectly simple: get online. The

online world, exactly like the real world, is crammed full of millions of people who'd love not to be single. Yes, some of them are mad. Yes, some of them are weird. Like I said, it's just like the real world. Develop radar and always trust your instinct. If you smell a rat, it's probably a rat. Don't give them the benefit of the doubt, and move on – otherwise you might end up like the late Elizabeth Jane Howard.[3]

5. **The way you develop radar is: practise**. Be careful to the point of paranoia with personal details on dating sites. Give a false name, if you like (you will need to create an email address in this name; it takes two seconds). Give a real, recent picture, obviously, and not one you've spent two hours Photoshopping – and remember, it's much, much better to be more attractive in the flesh, rather than a disappointment compared to

---

[3] When she was seventy-four, she was taken in by a con-man who wrote her a charming series of letters after she appeared on *Desert Island Discs*. She eventually met up with him. She'd been single for a long time and they had fantastic sex. He moved in. What happened next was, she later said in an interview, 'horrifying . . . he was a psychopath'. Her novel *Falling* provides a fictionalized account.

the retouched picture. Be absolutely honest about what you're looking for, but don't go overboard on superfluous personal specifics. 'I live in Central London' is fine; 'I live in Central London in a blue house with a red door just round the corner from a well-known restaurant' is not (I'm exaggerating, but you'd be amazed at what information people freely give out).

6. **Now write down a little bio describing what you're looking for.** My advice here is, keep it welcoming – not quite 'Greetings, all-comers! Over here!' but less 'Prince Millionaire Von Hottie, MD, PhD, QC'. Specificity is incredibly off-putting, not just to men but to human beings. Imagine how annoyed you'd feel if you read someone's bio and were made to feel too old, too short, too poor – and what can you do if your eye colour is wrong? So keep it elastic. This maximizes the number of replies you'll get, which maximizes choice. Don't sound dictatorial, it's really unsexy. Also, don't get too hung up on ages. It's possible to be a really active, handsome sixty-five and a totally boring arse at fifty.

7. **Our generation is the last one to think that dating sites are weird and**

for losers. I wouldn't dream of saying this (about them being 'for losers') in public, because lots of my friends are younger than me and in that age bracket – thirty-five to forty-five – where there isn't one friend who hasn't at some point met a partner online (and married them, in two cases). We, the older ones – The Older Ones! We should start a band – need to get rid of this prejudice. Online dating is now perfectly normal. More than that – it's the norm. You are not unique in your loneliness: it afflicts half the world. And since we're all busy and have finite time resources, online is not only sane but sensible. The alternative is like being one of my mothers-in-law, who once sadly exclaimed that 'my cuddling days are over'. Forget everything you think about tragic Lonely Hearts of yore. This is a whole new game, and normal people – people like you – play it, and win, every day.

8. **You should also think about non-dating sites.** I'm not suggesting you trawl these with a glint in your eye and friskiness on your mind, like a raptor, but it's obvious that a shared interest is an excellent starting point. If you love owls or *The Archers,* go and hang out

on their online forums. If you love fishing for pike, find a pike fishers' hangout. You never know – someone utterly charming-sounding might pop up.

9. **However, don't set too much store by 'shared interests'.** It can be much more interesting to be with someone whose interests are not identical to yours: you learn new stuff, for starters. I cautiously say that this can, sometimes, also apply to politics, provided you can keep the debate civilized. Putting 'no Tories' or 'no lefties' in any speculative online bio seems a bit jejune, to me.

10. **Non-dating sites include Twitter, Facebook and other social media.** Yes, parts of the internet are absolutely MAD. The thing is, it's very hard to hide who you really are on there. There do exist people who construct elaborate online personae, but they are not the norm. The norm are people like you or me, who just like chatting and jokes and knitting/*Game of Thrones*/dogs/whatever. After a while, you can tell a lot about a person by what they put online. If you like the cut of their jib, it's easy and un-weird to send them a one-liner suggesting you meet up for cake.

11. **Make new friends.** If you feel you'd like more friends, or that the friends you have are lovely but not much cop on the 'I feel like having a date' front, you're highly likely to meet some new ones online. These new friends will have friends of their own, and so on. If you're not the sort of person who is happy to find dates on the street – and I do see that not everyone is – expanding your social circle is the best thing you can do. And the most fun, too.

12. **A word of advice:** having opinions is interesting and nice; having shrieking, immutable views is less attractive, and hammering people over the head with these is not the way to make new friends. This is especially true of religion and politics (though see point 9 above). Saying something funny about a comical thing you've witnessed is good; oversharing – 'I feel so alone right now' – is a monumental turn-off.

13. **NB: Oversharing takes many forms,** which is to say that there are many ways of conveying that your life is more empty than you'd like. If you post something and nobody responds, don't post it again and again. Don't wail, 'Why is nobody responding?' The absolute golden rule of all online

activity is: don't be needy. And if you're needy – which we all are, up to a point (for approval, for confirmation or whatever) – learn to conceal it.

14. **As I keep saying, be elastic.** We're none of us spring chickens. People you date will be set in their ways, just as you are. They will have their own routines, their own ways of doing things, their own strongly expressed preferences. So will you. That's totally fine. But look at joggling along companionably here, rather than falling into the same groove. That might happen, but joggling is more likely, and joggling is nice.

15. **Safety is paramount:** never share any passwords; always let someone know where you are if you do meet people in the real world; meet in a public place; meet in daytime if you're anxious. But really, those are more disclaimers than advice: any encounters you do have are far more likely to be jolly than grim.

16. **It's important to realize that most people are nice, kind and good-hearted.** Really. We hear an awful lot about the nasty, monstrous ones that aren't, but most people just want to be cheerful and happy.

17. **Still don't fancy online dating?** That's fine, though you're missing out. Just remember that people who end up being significant in your life have a tendency to pop up out of nowhere, when you least expect them. This isn't to say that you should just stand there, waiting for the mountain to come to Mohammed: it helps to put yourself about a bit, in one way or another. All I'm saying is, hope springs eternal, and for very good reason.

Long-Term Singleness

Not everyone is roaming the streets looking for a partner or a fun night out – not everyone widowed is keen for Spouse Number 2, for example (though see page 170) – and despite my excellent advice above, it is true that not everyone who wants to pair up will succeed in doing so in the long term. We are a nation of lonely people, as the statistics cruelly remind us – among the loneliest in Europe, in fact.[4] Cherry on the cake

---

[4] In a June 2014 report from the Office for National Statistics, Britain was found to be one of the loneliest nations in Europe, with only Germans feeling more isolated and alone. We felt we had no one to turn to in a crisis; we felt that we were strangers within our own communities and had little sense of belonging; we were

of doom: it's bad for everyone, but it's *really* bad for old people.

BEING A MISTRESS

Look, it's really simple: if he wanted to be with you all the time, he'd leave his wife. But he's not going to, and there is, in the end, only one reason for this. It's not because he's waiting until the children are older. It's not because his wife is 'emotionally fragile'. It's because *he doesn't want to be with you all the time*. Because he likes being with her more. Personally – and I can only be subjective here – I would not want to be with anyone who didn't want to be with me all the time, unless I were Becky Sharp and trying to extract financial or social advantage from the situation, in which case good luck to hypothetical Becky Sharp me from 1847. Otherwise, though: nope.

Men who have long-term affairs are like greedy fat boys, feasting on double cream and then nipping out for custard: it's hard to see how this Two Dinners attitude is

---

unhappy with our social lives; and we felt unsafe at night. On the plus side, we were better off than the rest of Europe (counting our money alone, in our lonely street, crying).

considered sexy by anyone of sound mind. I'm not sitting in moral judgement here: if you're happy being someone's mistress, cool. But you're knocking on, time is passing, and life is short.

The maddening thing is, we all know about the isolation of old age. We all flinch when we hear yet another absolutely shocking story of abuse in care homes. We change the channel uneasily when a television report comes up on the same subject, or we force ourselves to watch and have nightmares for three days. It's partly because we have, or did have, or soon will have, aged parents (see chapter 6), but it's also because we're all headed in one direction, and one direction only. And one of the reasons that we may have difficulty coping with the idea of this – of age, and decrepitude, and decay – is that everywhere you turn, you see such an utterly bloody grim depiction of it.

There are things that can't be helped – memory loss, dementia, aggressive illnesses. Of the rest, though, many *can* be helped. There is no need to sit there a-tremble, wondering what will become of you when you get really old – a fear that's pretty bad for most of us and that must be even more acute for somebody who is single with no dependants. I have two solutions to offer, and I think they're really good ones, and after that I have an 'umble third suggestion.

Podding Up

First, I'd like to write about **the not-so-ancient**. Say you're in your mid-fifties, or sixties – not absolutely antique, let's say. And say, because it's relevant here, that you either never had children or that your children are grown-up rather than little – grown-up enough to have left home. And say that your house is a bit too big for you, and say that property prices are mad (as they are at the time of writing). And say that you have several friends – or even just one – in the same boat. Why on earth wouldn't you pool resources and live together? Loneliness, the modern disease, is corrosive and devastating. Why, when there is a simple solution, would you not take it? Give a room or two, or a floor or two, of the flat/house to a friend in the same boat, and just like that you are no longer two lonely little barks bobbing along in the giant sea, but a two-berth vessel. (I am planning to expand this model in older old age – less the two-berth vessel, more the frigate.)

It doesn't mean that you have to spend every waking hour together. But my goodness, how nice to come home and smell cooking, because one of you has made supper. How nice to swap book recommendations, to have somebody to yell at the television with, to go to a show or an exhibition with, to ask for help with the crossword. Alone when you want to be, with company when not. If you don't have a friend of a similar age to pod up with, then do consider someone older, like a companion in a novel by the sainted Barbara Pym. It used to be that single women were always having nieces and the grown-up children of friends – or of friends of friends – lodging with them. That doesn't seem to happen any more, and I think it's a terrible shame.

Communal Living

I'm not talking sheltered housing or old people's home here, but rather **DIY old people's communes**. The truth of the matter is that the couples model is outdated and old-fashioned, for the very good reason that the uncoupled are just as numerous as the coupled-up. Fifty-one per cent of us are single, divorced, widowed or have never married (a figure that's gone up from 47 per cent in the past decade).[5] What do you do if you have lots of people who are friends and don't wish to spend their later years alone? You put them together, obviously.

Some friends and I are going to sell our various houses and buy one huge house at the seaside instead, in which we'll have spacious apartments. There will be a bar and a restaurant downstairs. There might even be a barn with a medical wing in it. We'll play poker and drink

[5] Report by the Office for National Statistics, following the 2011 census.

cocktails, garden and draw, go for walks and play bridge. It'll be a version of sheltered housing, with the freedom to be alone but the knowledge that, if you want to hang out, your friends are all at hand. There may be a reciprocal arrangement with a similar commune in London, which another friend is setting up, for when we fancy trips down to town.

For all I know, such communes exist already – I hope so, at any rate, because they're a brilliant idea: sometimes, it really does literally take a village. They rather remind me of squats in eighties London – except salubrious, prosperous, and with no need to label your shelf of the fridge with passive-aggressive messages ('This is Beast's hummus, do not touch'). They're a bit like student halls, too, crossed with a fantasy farmhouse. Living communally is really fun: people need people, and as long as said people have enough space, well, it's really hard to see the flaw in the plan. (I do see it: it's what to do if and when people get seriously ill – iller than the medical barn can cope with. But there's a way around that. You just stick a clause in the contract you sign when you join the commune, saying: 'If the barn medics can't help me, I agree to live somewhere with better medical facilities.')

A Quick Word about Spinsters

Spinster! The very word is like a knell. Now, it used to be that spinsters had a really nice life.

They lived together, as spinsters, usually in quite a modest and bookish way – though obviously neither bookishness nor modesty are prerequisites. Nobody thought it peculiar, and certainly nobody constantly asked the spinsters if they were lesbians (which they may have been in some instances, I suppose, and which makes me feel pleased for them, all sneaky and lezzo on the sly). Anyway, I humbly suggest the word – so appallingly pejorative – should be reclaimed, and I think that spinsters should be proud of their spinsterhood.

Some women are perfectly happy to live quite dry, correct, uncomplicated lives: not everybody roams the land wailing about boyfriends and worrying about looking like mutton, thank God. Some people are by nature more ascetic than others, and I wish they'd just come out and be good and spinsterish when they feel like it, instead of only embracing the spinsterishness when they hit, say, sixty. Some people are born spinsters and like it that way. Good luck to 'em.

TAKING UP WITH A MUCH YOUNGER MAN

. . . who you met in Turkey or Morocco, inevitably. So handsome. Such a gifted linguist. No, no, nobody's sniggering: what you have is indeed special, to you. (I mean this. Sod other people.) Now, this doesn't look great: the sixty-year-old, madly in love

– actually, 'madly in sex', which really ought to be a phrase – with the 23-year-old Turkish hottie, who – my God, has the world gone mad? – she is proposing to MARRY and BRING OVER HERE. (Terribly embarrassing for her thirty-something children, though I note that women who do this are almost always childless; ditto absurd so-called cougars.)

But do you know what? It can work. It's basically a financial transaction – the woman, who is never poor, sets the guy up with a restaurant or a bar, or some other business, and in exchange for this, he sleeps with her. They have a jolly time for a few years, and then he goes back to Turkey or Morocco and marries someone his age. If you are able to see it for what it is – which is paid sex, rather than Abelard and Heloise – it's fine. It's not my cup of tea, but it's hard to see the harm. Also – who knows? – one day it might turn out that one of these guys is a genuine, bona fide gerontophile, so, er . . . yay.

Getting Back into the Dating Game

OK, so let's assume that you wanted a boyfriend and have, cleverly, found yourself one. Now what? It may be years since you dated; it may be that you find yourself slightly baffled by the ever-shifting conventions of the dating world. Cheer up: the principle remains the same, except with more texts.

SEX AFTER A DROUGHT

The idea of this is a great deal more agitating than the reality. Nobody forgets how to have sex, so that's good. Also, the reality is that if you fancy somebody, and they fancy you, then you will both be pleased and excited to find yourselves naked in a bed.

Men don't stop having a boner because your tummy sticks out or your bottom is saggy or you're sixty-four.

They're just really pleased to be about to have sex.

With you.

All old and naked.

Hurrah!

CHAPTER 4

FAMILY RELATIONSHIPS

Parenting teenagers, stepchildren, blended families, the whole shebang

Deep breath – *sticks head between legs* – right, here we go.
Parenting older children can, for prolonged periods of time, be a bit (ha, 'a bit', hahaha) of a nightmare. This is why I don't go a giant bundle on very old first-time mothers – though good luck to them, each to her own, etc. It's not the idea of having a baby at forty-six that bothers me – it's the sheer lunacy of thinking that, when that child is sixteen, and wild, and you're sixty-two, SIXTY-TWO, you're going to be ideally placed to set boundaries, impose order on the chaos that seems to arise every couple of days, and parent a young adult who thinks themselves too old to be parented, especially by a nan (sorry). Seriously, and I mean this from the heart, absolutely best of luck with that. I was forty-one when my elder son was sixteen and his brother was thirteen, I have nerves of steel and the determination of a mule, and I found it . . . quite arduous, let's say.

The great, stupid, insulting **lie about parenting** is that the first years are tough, and that if you somehow power through those, you're on the home run: that it all gets easier. This is a load of absolute steaming horseshit, though I suppose that if baby manuals said, 'This is the piece-of-cake bit that we will look back on with longing,' people would stick to only having one child and the human race would eventually die out – or turn into China, or something. But anyway: it's true. The sleepless, puke-on-your-shoulder, toddler-tantrum years are the easiest bit. It gets so much harder. The good news is, the hard bit ends. Eventually. (It's amazing that new parents don't realize this. Do they not remember being a teenager?)

So if you're a woman who's had a child very late, please bear this in mind when you chat to us, the walking wounded, the veterans of a couple of tours of teenagehood and beyond. It's not that we're being unsympathetic if we appear to be unresponsive when you moan for hours about teething ('Yeah? Try Bonjela'). It's that we have a fifteen-year-old bursting with hormones and naughtiness and curiosity, loose on the street when they should have been home an hour ago. It's that we exist in a constant state of panic about sex, drugs, alcohol, school, boys, girls, pregnancy, STDs, bullying, eating disorders, body image, bad friends, bad grown-ups, etc., etc., etc. You are yoked to a baby or toddler. We are yoked to an adult – or two, or three. And it's much, *much* harder.

118

WHAT TO DO WHEN YOU'RE NO LONGER THE BOSS

The window of you being the boss of children, and of them listening, and looking at you with big 'my mummy knows everything' eyes, is *tiny*. You, of course, don't realize this. You carry merrily on, feeling pleased with yourself that everything is more or less shipshape, and then, when your child is around thirteen, you realize that your time is up. The wheels start falling off as the date approaches, and suddenly – wham, that's it – it's gone. Goodbye blissful, unquestioned authority. The eyes aren't agape with adoring wonderment any more: your children have discovered that you are fully fallible, and tiresomely they equate this with the need to question *everything*. There is no more bossing, only bargaining, of the kind that would try the patience of professional hostage negotiators – and you're not a negotiator, just a parent trying to get by as best she can.

I say this, by the way, as the mother of two extremely nice adult men, of whom I am enormously proud, and whose teenagehoods were nowhere near the nightmare that some of my friends and their kids went through. I say this as someone who was *lucky*. (My daughter's only ten, so I'm still on relatively safe ground there. That's a thing, though, with big gaps: parenting teenagers at the same time as a two-year-old is *a little bit tiring*.)

119

The difficulty with parenting this age group is that they don't want parenting or bossing – they do not accept that it is needed any longer. This means adopting other strategies: becoming wilier. **You need wiles**. Oh, how you need wiles. Because, crucially, these children still need both **parenting and boundaries**. Giving in can seem tempting – and sometimes people do: they just give up and go, 'You're six foot tall, you shave, you look like an adult even though you're not – you know what? Go for it. Fuck it. I'm tired; I honestly don't think I can hack this *and* work *and* running the house *and* looking after my ailing mother *and* the nine million other things going on in my life.' In actual fact, giving in is a catastrophe. By doing so you are effectively giving up on parenting, which is not only reprehensible and sad but which – in my actually quite considerable experience of fucked-uppery – tends not to end well.

I know lots of kids, both in my generation and in my children's, who were effectively left to their own devices very young. They made all the mistakes. Of course, we all make loads of mistakes – but the difference is, those kids didn't have parents who picked them up when they fell. By the time they noticed there was a problem, the problem was too entrenched to be properly grasped. The parents parented when they paid for rehab, though, which was nice of them. Some of them still pay for the ongoing therapy of people old enough to have children themselves.

Setting Boundaries

So the burning question is: how to set them? What do you say when 'be in by 10 p.m.' is just a meaningless string of words to be ignored at will, which you may as well be delivering in Xhosa or Zulu? Here are some tips. Man, these tips were hard-earned:

* **This is not the time to start thinking, 'Aw, she's more like my mate than my daughter/ he's my pal.'** I mean, I absolutely am friends with my children, and have always been friends with them. (I could, and do, reduce myself to tears thinking about their dearest woolly hats, their duffel coats, their little mittened hands, holding mine so tightly, one on each side, three abreast going for chips on a dark winter's night.) So of course, *of course*, I'm their friend to the death. But above all that, I am their mother. Being their friend was never the most important thing to me; I wanted to be strong enough to be the police when I needed to be. The 'We're mates, aren't we?' thing is both grossly needy on the parental side (plus it contains a creepy element of 'I'm still young. Aren't I? Aren't I? Hey, let's swap clothes!') and a convenient abnegation of responsibility. I prefer 'I'm your mum'. My children and I have tons of friends. I only have three children, and they only have one mum.

121

* **Being the police is especially – desperately, actually – important if you are a single parent.** It is also violently counter-intuitive: what parent in her right mind sets out to be occasionally disliked by her own children? Whose natural inclination isn't for an easy life? But I'm afraid you have to bite the bullet. Sometimes you will say a thing and be disliked for it. No child deserves a wet rag of a mother they can run rings around; no male child deserves to be taught that women are weak, wobbly or easily manipulated. You need to say No when you need to say No. Obviously you're only the police some of the time – it's not like the house suddenly becomes a police state.

* **In separated families, the absent parent is often the 'nice' one** – the spoiling one, the one who puts his or her head to the side and says, 'Yes, that does sound unreasonable, I'll have a word with him/her.' This is understandable, but it's a real fucker, and terribly (not deliberately, usually) undermining. You need to present a united front at all times where at all humanly possible. 'We both agree that you can't go to the mixed sleepover in the empty house, because you're twelve.' And that is that.

* **In families that are together, that scenario presents itself as well** – often, though by no means always, along gender lines. The spikiness

122

occurs between a girl and her mother; the girl turns to her father for succour; ditto with boys and mothers. Again, I would strongly caution against 'allowing' your co-parent to 'take charge' of a particular situation, and would always emphasize the superiority of a solution that's reached together, as a joint enterprise. This way you avoid the 'My dad's very strict, but my mum's a pushover' – or vice versa – scenario. It's a scenario that's not only unhelpful but that also stays put into adulthood. If you're the pushover, you'll be seen as a bit wet until your dying day, even when your kids have kids of their own, and even though you may not be remotely wet. If you're the dragon, you'll be seen as the dragon for evermore. This isn't good, or helpful, and when your grandchildren come along, they will subliminally be raised to think of you as a wet flannel/dragon lady. Bad.

* **Think of the messages you are giving your children about men and women,** because those messages are very powerful and stay with kids for life. Too often, and despite our best intentions, we may veer into 'women are irrational and shouty, men are sane and calm' territory. You do *not* want to raise those sorts of boys. Nor do you want to raise daddy's girls who are a bit flirty and manipulative around older men – especially if those girls have male teachers.

* **Do not feel more isolated than you need to be.** Always communicate. I think we all probably have a story about being asked to a party when we were in our teens, and how we nearly died of shame because our mum rang their mum to ask exactly what the set-up was. It's a funny old day when you realize that you are in fact your mum, and feel no embarrassment whatsoever about making exactly the same phone call. Here's the funny thing, though: you ring around, and you find you aren't alone, and then you discover that the other parents are also quite freaked out about fifteen-year-old Alice being left alone in the house for the weekend and inviting a load of rowdy older boys to the sleepover. And the parents chat to each other, and the mixed sleepover becomes girls only – and the problem is solved.

* **Always, always keep the lines of communication with your children wide open,** even if you're absolutely enraged by them and their stupid behaviour, even if you are incandescent with fury. 'Because I say so' doesn't cut it any more – but neither do sulking, sarcasm, anger, bitchiness or silence. Always choose diplomacy instead of all-out war, even if you really have to force yourself and wouldn't at all mind deploying your heavy artillery, and then some. Talking solves most things. Eventually.

124

* **Accept that you probably won't get your way every time.** Always be open to compromise. The urge to bang your gavel is omnipresent, and there will be moments when the bench is all yours. But pick them well: insisting on your own way is only effective if it's occasional. Too many bangs with the gavel and you're just white noise.

* **It is wholly acceptable, when offered unsolicited parenting advice by people who have never had children, to tell them to piss off.** I don't care if they have nephews or nieces – no, actually, it's not remotely 'the same', or even very roughly equivalent. People who haven't had kids have absolutely no right to voice any kind of opinion *at all* about how other people should or shouldn't raise their children, because they know jackshit.[1] Everybody thinks this, and we're all too nice to say. Seriously: pipe down. (And see below for more on this very thing in the context of step-parenting.)

Additionally, I have some cheering thoughts. Difficult – difficult to you – children (and I include mouthy, recalcitrant ones, unconventional ones,

---

[1] Unless they have spent decades as a professional nanny, or in loco parentis. Sole exception. And even then, only sometimes.

problem ones, eccentric ones), are often intelligent children who are just demonstrating a curious, questioning mind and a curious, questioning approach to the world. That's going to turn out to be a good thing in the long run, though maybe it doesn't feel like that when they are eleven and view arguing you to a standstill as some kind of Olympic sport.

Also, it doesn't hurt to occasionally remind yourself of how crappy it is being a teenager, stuck in a sort of limbo, neither quite one thing nor the other, beset by all sorts of anxieties. Beneath the swagger and the noise and dickery is a child – more often than not, a child who's feeling a bit lost.

Balancing Fear with Fairness

I've saved my best and most helpful (to me) piece of advice until now. It is this. Teenagers have a strong sense of natural justice, and an equally strong bullshit detector. I can remember, and I'm sure you can too, occasions when, as a teenager myself, I felt absolutely decimated by the unfairness of a decision, either at home or at school. I *knew* that this time, this once, I wasn't pushing my luck or being cheeky – I was being reasonable, and my parent's or teacher's response was just plain unfair. It used to make me feel like my universe had been rocked, because I expected my parents/teachers to be annoying, too strict, or whatever – but not to take mad-seeming, arbitrary, *irrational* decisions that made no sense at all.

As parents, we know that anger and fear are two sides of the same coin. When we're very angry at our child, we're usually also very frightened. For example: you don't seriously mind about the actual *time* if your fifteen-year-old daughter says she will be home at ten in the evening and arrives at midnight. You mind about what might have happened to her in those two hours. You are frightened for her, imagining terrible things, awful things that you can't push out of your head. You're pacing up and down looking at the clock, and you're beside yourself – not because it's twelve o'clock at night, but because it's dark and the world can be a bad place. She comes in cheerfully, shouts through that her phone ran out of charge but that they'd all gone for a pizza after the film, then comes into the kitchen to find you white-faced and spluttering with anger.

'You're grounded for a month!' you yell before even saying hello, because all of that fear has turned into fury.

Your daughter looks at you uncomprehendingly. 'What, because I went for a pizza?'

'Don't answer back,' you shout, and so on.

'Why are you shouting?' she asks.

'I'm not shouting,' you bellow.

Your daughter's feelings of confusion are perfectly legitimate here. You're the one behaving like a nutter, and she knows it. But she also knows that if she tries to point it out to you, you're in such a state that you might threaten to ground her for *a year*. So she says nothing – or nothing too awful – and goes to bed feeling sad and puzzled, her evening ruined.

The disproportionate freak-out is bad, but it's not as bad as the other really terrible thing, which is saying something bitchy – being a bitch – to your own child. Now you are not only being completely over the top, but you're also being foul – fouler than you would ever be to a friend or colleague, let alone to someone who is a child.

The point is, it's absolutely fine to feel precarious as a parent, it's fine to massively overreact, and fine to get it wrong – even fine to be a bit nasty. Who doesn't sometimes do these things? But it is really, really important, when you have massively overreacted – or got it wrong or bitched – to apologize. We've all shouted completely over-the-top things at our children, in a state of fear, rage or stress. Where we know those things to be unreasonable – borderline mad, sometimes – it is our job to redeem ourselves, by saying sorry.

In the example above, the child no longer goes to bed confused and unhappy. You say, 'I'm so sorry, I totally lost the plot there – of course you're not grounded for a month. I just hate not knowing where you are, it really makes me anxious – maybe we could go and get a spare phone battery tomorrow.' And now things are fine. You have explained yourself, you have apologized and you have retrieved the situation. Your daughter goes to bed happy, and doesn't lie there in the dark thinking, 'My mother is mad and I hate her.'

Don't become some cringing wreck who says 'sorry, sorry, sorry' when there's no need to. But on those occasions when you know – and your child knows, and everybody knows – that you've been grossly, bang-out-of-order unfair, apologize. As well as being the right thing to do, saying sorry saves so much trouble in the long run. And you can't be expected to hold any kind of moral authority at all if you're seen to be unjust.

NOT GOT TEENAGERS YET?

Here's everything I've learned about parenting younger children:

* **Do what works for you.** Never feel bad about it.

* **Manners are unbelievably important** – today, tomorrow and for evermore. Don't raise a child who has awful manners. It's not fair on them.

* **Manners turn into charm.** Charm is more precious than gold – and it's acquired, not taught.

* **Tell your children off if they misbehave.** Don't be the sort of doting imbecile who thinks

rudeness is 'funny'. No one will like your kids, and your kids will suffer.

* **Don't inflict tired children on your friends.** If your small children are badly behaved and your excuse is that they're 'tired', put them to bed.

* **All children take mad liberties, in order to test boundaries.** Provide those boundaries. They usually require you saying a clear and emphatic 'no'.

* **Going to bed at a decent hour is essential during term time.** Not everyone is charmed by children rampaging at 11 p.m., even out of term time. There's nothing wrong with the notion of child-free grown-up time.

* **Never treat your child as a lifestyle accessory.** Kids playing in pubs while the adults get pissed may be convenient for you, but you can't look after them properly if your attention is focused on your mates/wine.

* **All healthy children learn to walk, talk and use the lavatory.** Getting competitive about when this happens is absurd.

* **All healthy older children learn to read, write and do homework.** There's no need to get competitive about this either.

* **No one cares if your child is gifted or talented or has the vocabulary of an Oxford don.** All other people care about is that your child is nice to be around. That includes 'not weird'.

* **Lots of kids *are* weird.** It is especially important to make sure that these kids are well socialized. Weird and poorly socialized is an unhappy combo, in childhood and beyond.

* **If you have the strong sense that your child is more than ordinarily weird,** never delay getting a diagnosis for reasons of social embarrassment or stigma. These do not help the child.

* **School work is important,** but it's not the be-all and end-all.

* **Activities outside the classroom are just as important** – knowing the names of trees, looking at fossils and going to museums cheerfully, to list just a few.

* **As is enthusiasm** – about anything at all, whether you approve or disapprove of it.

* **A child who is 'arty' or sporty rather than academic does not have to be excused or explained away.** He or she is a joy. Art and sports are *talents*.

*   **A nice child is a child who is nice to other children,** especially younger ones.

*   **Tutoring fucks a lot of children up.** Not all of them. But . . .

*   **. . . it is rarely worth it.** (See also the kind of 'activity' calendar that allows no free time to mooch about or daydream in.)

*   **Boredom is necessary:** it encourages imagination and teaches self-reliance.

*   **Sometimes 'malingering' is actually appendicitis.** I have learned this at first hand.

*   **The nicest children are always a little bit shy;** the least appealing are (sometimes almost grotesquely) over-confident.

*   **Don't see your children as a malleable version of your younger self,** to be 'improved' accordingly. Such parents often have really unhappy children. It's sad that you're sad about the fact that you didn't go to Oxford, for instance. But it's even sadder to train up your only averagely academic son from the age of eight with the specific aim of him going for you.

That last point has loads of applications (and see the Good Child, page 139). Does your child genuinely love practising the bassoon for two hours every night, or do you love being the mother of a Grade 8 bassoonist more? At the other end of the scale, is it nice for your twelve-year-old to model, or do you like the idea that your genes produced a beauty?

A NOTE ON CHARM

Fact: being charming gets you everywhere, and pretty much always gets you what you want, within reason. I note, and have been noting for the past twenty years – hoiking my bosoms and doing disapproving huffs – that an awful lot of children and teenagers are really, really uncharming. It's an especially middle-class problem, and is particularly true of children who work incredibly hard, have loads of after-school activities but don't necessarily spend a great deal of time with adults who aren't parents or teachers, or with kids they don't know outside school or from the queue for Mandarin lessons. Lots of children are terrible at making small talk with adults they might come across at home or out on visits, but I'm thinking here about kids of ten and upwards who are articulate and clever enough not to sit there silently, like puddings. An ability to make small talk is one of the things that makes you charming. Making small talk also shows that you have been brought up nicely, and therefore have manners.

Small talk does not have to be dazzlingly insightful, or even clever. What it does have to be is non-needy: 'I got 96 per cent in my French exam, you know' is not charming, because it expects the verbal equivalent of a pat on the head. But 'Are you having a nice time? I am, because . . .' is charming and engaging. So are:

- **asking questions**
- **showing interest in other people and their lives,** and
- **volunteering opinions** (up to a point: it helps if the opinions are not of the 'I really hate your dog' variety).

Basically, showing human curiosity and human delight in things is charming. Sitting there mutely is not. Also, this kind of chat teaches kids how to read people and situations, which comes in very handy in their immediate, child-centred world – as well as standing them in good stead when they become adults.

You can't teach charm, but you *can* teach manners, and everybody should.

SURVIVING TEENAGEHOOD

Now then, teenagers. Here is what is ordinarily naughty and not really worth freaking out about:

* **Occasional rudeness.** It goes with the territory.

* **Occasional underage drinking, in groups.** Illegal, mind you. I would hate to encourage anyone to break the law, or indeed urge any parent to encourage underage drinking, but it's probably going to happen anyway. For what it's worth, better it takes place in your garden (i.e. outdoors, in case of vomit) where you can keep a disapproving eye on it, rather than round the back of some dodgy car park. Yes, this does put you in quite a morally dubious position, but it seems the best compromise.

* **Occasional experimentation with drugs.** Ditto. If my kid's going to be slightly wasted with his mates, I do not want him or her clambering up some scaffolding to dance on a roof at the other end of town. I want 'em all where I can see the whites (reds) of their eyes when I storm up to their bedroom, coughing ostentatiously, to tell them off.

* **Having boyfriends/girlfriends.** This in itself isn't 'naughty' at all, but there is the question of what they get up to below the age of sixteen;

as you will be aware, a boy can sleep with his girlfriend when she is two days short of her sixteenth birthday and technically be charged with statutory rape. It is a really good idea to spell this out to children of both genders extremely clearly and explicitly. In terms of boyfriends visiting, I think it is always better if the boy visits the girl's house, because at least you know exactly where your daughter is. Also, I don't care if they have PSE at school: never shy away from the contraception chat. If teenagers are old enough to have sex, they're old enough to know how not to get pregnant.

*   **Bunking off school once or twice.** It happens. It's really annoying, but it happens.

*   **Having an experience of shoplifting;** hopefully not being caught. Ditto.

*   **Having an unmanageably large party,** when you make the fatal mistake (not a mistake you make twice) of going away for the weekend.

*   **Having a fight,** so that you have to go into school and stand there while your son or daughter apologizes to the other son or daughter for whacking them.

Here is what I would consider problematically naughty:

* **Being rude all the time.** I mean, *all the time*. Sometimes it feels like it's all the time, but it's really not. Rude all the time means anger issues; these might (will) need addressing.

* **Underage drinking solo.** Drinking alone is never a good sign, including in adulthood. In teenagers, it may be a sign of depression.

* **Taking a lot of drugs,** especially taking a lot of drugs alone. Self-explanatory, one would hope.

* **Having a very high turnover on the boyfriend/girlfriend front and finding it amusing.** There's a difference between feeling giddy at the idea of pairing up and feeling despotic (sociopathic) about the feeling of power this gives. Playing around with people's feelings is not a thing that should be encouraged. Fathers who call their sons 'lads' when they manifest zero respect for their ever-changing rota of girlfriends: don't encourage it. Girls who date boys only to make fun of them afterwards: frown upon it.

* **Having no girlfriend/boyfriend at all, ever.** Not 'naughty' but quite weird, in this age range: it might be worth having a word in case this has to do with issues of self-worth/self-esteem/confused sexuality.

* **Bunking off school habitually/refusing to go to school.** One of my boys did this. It drove me NUTS. He insisted that he was done and was ready for a job; eventually I agreed, and he went and worked for a year. After that, he announced – of his own free will – that he was ready to go back to school for A-levels. Hold your nerve: it usually works out fine. But don't ignore it, or think it's a phase. Of course it may be that there's stuff happening at school that your child really doesn't like. (By the way, there's nothing wrong with leaving school at sixteen if you're hungry and ambitious and know where you're heading. It's the great, pointless middle-class educational taboo.)

* **Habitual shoplifting,** for obvious reasons. (I did this as a teenager. Why? Because I could; because the kids I was friends with all shoplifted too; because I was bored and unhappy. Mostly the latter.) Again, have a word – not a shouted, condemnatory word: a conversation.

* **Appearing not to have a social life.** Not naughty either, but if it's really an absolute desert, then cause for concern.

* **Fighting all the time/bullying other kids.** Not OK, ever. Something's gone badly awry and you need to get on it right away.

Here's another cheering thing: ordinarily naughty teenagers, and even problematically naughty ones, are usually done with the naughtiness by the time they go to university. This is brilliant news. I'd taken a lot of drugs and slept with a lot of boys by the time I went to mine, so that when I arrived I had little interest in spending my time being an arse. Compare and contrast with young people who haven't had the freedom to experiment a little bit: they go completely mad, make passes at anything that moves, drink themselves into a stupor, choke on their own vomit, view members of the opposite sex with a sort of wild, boggle-eyed surmise that is massively off-putting, and are generally viewed with utter contempt by the people who were annoying, risk-taking, parent-dementing teenagers. Every cloud.

The Good Child

Perhaps you're reading all this and thinking, 'Blimey, my child would never do any of the things described in this chapter – not one.' Well, that's nice – and good for you, probably. But a) are you really sure about that? And b) before we put out the bunting, let me acquaint you with my theory concerning the Good Child.

First, some children just *are* good, or at least 'good-er' than their contemporaries (I'm on teenage children here, not small children) – and jolly nice they are, too. Well done.

139

But the ones in my theory are *too* good. They're gentle and kind and they want nothing more than to please their parents and fulfil all their hopes and expectations. They are polite, pleasant, quiet, often self-effacing but always happy to 'perform', like little seals. They rarely moan or complain – and why should they? Everything about their life feels ordered and ordained. They're like those battery-operated toys that you set on a track – a toy train, say (though my daughter had some bug-like creatures that did the same thing) – and off they go, so valiantly, so diligently, round the track, and round the track, and round the track again.

HOW TO SPOT THE GOOD CHILD

The Good Child really loves her parents, and she – because she's almost always a she – is at her happiest when she has made them proud. For some reason, the parents aren't automatically proud all the time – or if they are, they don't necessarily convey it, or if they convey it, then it's not clear enough. But they are made vocally and demonstrably proud by achievements, by sticky stars on charts, by prizes, by cups, by awards – by excellence, in short. And that's absolutely fine, of course – what parent isn't made happy by a sticky star?

There are some problems with the Good Child:

- **Her sense of worth is tied in entirely with her academic achievements,** because her academic achievements are how she defines herself. That isn't ideal. She's fourteen: she should have her own way of defining herself by now – a way that has nothing to do with parental expectations. It doesn't have to be clever or sophisticated. Lots of fourteen-year-olds define themselves by their friends, the clothes they wear and the music they listen to. Yes, it's shallow. So what? They're allowed: they're fourteen. Instead, the Good Child defines herself by what she's achieved. She's pleased with herself because of all the A grades, but she is angry with herself too, because she can't get above a B in Chemistry. She tries all the time but it's not enough: she must try harder.

- **She is desperate to make her parents happy.** I repeat – she's a teenager. She should be going through a narcissistic and experimental period, flicking meta-phorical (ideally) V-signs, not sitting at home loving her parents and doing extra Maths. And what's going on in her head? Does she think that unless she is excellent, unless she excels, she's somehow unworthy? Why is she even anxious about that? Parents love their children, even their annoying teenage ones: it's unconditional and we can't help it. What is it about this girl, this good girl, this exemplar, that has caused her to feel that she needs to keep performing, winning, excelling, to be sure of her parents' love? Why is she so desperate to please? And why don't her parents see how weird this is, and how uncertainly it might end?

I knew several girls like this when I was at boarding school, and really, even at fifteen, you hardly needed a doctorate in psychology to work out what was going on. Those good girls, those dedicated, hard-working, uncomplaining girls, worked so hard to impress their parents in the vain and tragic hope that, if they showed themselves to be good – so quiet, so nice, so clever, no trouble at all! – they might be allowed to live at home, with their mother and father, like normal girls.[2] It's more poignant than I can bear, actually, and occasionally, thirty-five years later, I recognize a version of the same thing in a teenage girl I meet. Something is terribly the matter inside them – something is terribly sad, far sadder than it has any right to be in someone who is still a child.

Often, it's wanting to live with both parents,

[2] It never worked.

in a situation where that's not possible due to divorce or separation. Even more often, it's an attempt at trying to fix things (like turning yourself into a human plaster). Where the family situation is complicated, unclear or chaotic, or where it is somewhere on the scale from mildly unhappy to absolutely terrible, the Good Child attempts to make things better through the medium of her own excellence. 'Look,' she is saying, 'I'm over here, I got 99 per cent in my test. Everything will be all right, won't it? I got 99 per cent. I'm making everything fine. I love you! Please love me back.' (Sometimes it's not that at all: sometimes the child sees education as ammunition, and is gathering up as much as she can before heading for the door, never to return. But that's more likely to be the case in profoundly unhappy, messed-up families where professional expectations are historically low.)

It sometimes becomes clearer and clearer, as she heads into adolescence, that the Good Child (and, let's face it, she was trained to be good by one or both parents; children are born wild little anarchists) is good but unhappy. Put it this way: the Good Child is the classic candidate for eating disorders and for very specific mental disorders such as OCD. Go to any eating disorder facility – and I've been to several in the course of my life (as an observer, not as an inmate) – and you see them all. So clever. So high achieving. So middle class. So good. So unhappy.

Look, you may just have an adorable child, who was born good and was always good and will remain good, because good is what they are. But all kids are good. The definition of 'good' that I'm using with my hypothetical girl is very specific: it's the kind of good that doesn't always come naturally, the good that needs, literally, to be taught. I'm very, very wary of it, and I think everyone should keep an eye out for it. Sometimes really, really good is very bad.

And another thing: nobody can maintain that level of excellence forever. You see those kids at university, appalled at – as they see it – losing their place in the world, wandering about like they've lost their footing. Because if they aren't top of the class any more, then who on earth are they, and what are they *for*?

NB: It is a kindness to say to children, always, 'I'll be really pleased if you do brilliantly, but to be absolutely honest, it's not that important. I'd rather you were happy.'

The Pleaser

A less extreme version of the Good Child is the Pleaser. She's the child – again, she's usually a girl – all the other parents envy you for.

HOW TO SPOT THE PLEASER

The Pleaser doesn't have the fairly brooding intensity of the Good Child and is much better at functioning socially: she has lots of friends and can be the life and soul. She's just lovely. Couldn't be nicer, kinder, friendlier, more helpful. And so accomplished! Unlike the Good Child, who can seem shy or withdrawn, the Pleaser is comfortable with finding herself the centre of attention; she may even, in childhood, be a bit of a show-off.

The problem with the Pleaser is that her main driver is fear of rejection (in adulthood, this sometimes translates into Pleasers being extraordinarily pushy and ambitious, though Pleasers are more often a little bit wet and a little bit passive-aggressive). The even greater problem is that we inadvertently raise most girls to be Pleasers, not least because our entire culture is so complicit that it can happen just by osmosis: are you thin enough, pretty enough, blonde enough, cute enough? Enough for what, though? It's never made explicit, but surely the answer is 'enough to be unthreatening, malleable, a pushover'.

Keep an eye out, because underneath all that pleasing, she is intensely self-critical and constantly measuring her worth. (Adult

Pleasers, by the way, are crippled by their need to be liked, to be good, to be seen to do the right thing. It's half a cry for help and half a cry for love – either way, it's not something you'd wish your child to have to deal with.)

My theory is that this is all to do with girls and their dads. We all know dads who are strong characters – forces of nature, often, ultra-charming and charismatic – who are quite keen on the old 'constructive criticism'. This is another term for home truths, delivered in the spirit of tough love, but truths that carry a sting with them – and often a devastating one, if you're sensitive and aged ten. The question here is: 'Are you clever/pretty/sporty/polite enough to please *me*? Because I may temporarily withdraw my love or approbation if you're not.' And then when the child pleases the parent, the love comes back – and how delicious, how golden, how wonderful it feels.

But then my theory is based on the fact that I am a *dis*pleaser – I couldn't give a flying fuck about any of this stuff. (I say this matter-of-factly, not proudly. It's just a thing about me, like having black hair.) I think that this is because the idea of pleasing my father never entered my head, mostly because my parents had broken up when I was two and he lived in another country. He seemed very pleased with me as I was: I never had the sense that he'd have been more pleased if I were different. I also think this has informed all my relationships with men, by the way, and explains why I find men so easy to be around: I was not brought up with the sense that they were creatures to please and impress, nor was I expected to modify my behaviour for them. And I did not spend any of my childhood seeking male approval.

Anyway, let's return to the Pleaser. For one reason or another – and it could be her mother she is trying so hard to please, not just her dad, or, in a joyous double whammy, it could be both – she feels that love does not flow freely but is like a tap. Do something great and, whoosh – out it flows. Sit around not doing anything in particular and, oh dear – no water.

Now, of course, we as parents feel extra-loving when our child has done something marvellous, but it is important for children to understand that love is not conditional, and that they are loved, through gritted teeth, even when they're being atrocious little (or big) shites.

Gender-Specific Anxieties about Teenagers

Most parental anxieties – drinking, drugs, sex – are equal-opportunities anxieties. Two aren't:

* **fighting and violence** with boys, and

* **unwelcome male attention** with girls.

This isn't to say that girls don't fight, or that boys don't ever get unwelcome male – or female – attention. But by and large, if it's two in the morning and your child is making their way back from a party, those are your (main) anxieties as a parent. Will he get into a fight, will he be the target of violence, will someone mad appear and bottle him? Will she be OK walking about looking like that, dressed like that? What if someone follows her? What if someone pulls her into a car? Why wouldn't she let me collect her?

It's worse with girls. It just is. Girls are vulnerable in a way that boys are not. Both my boys have been mugged at knifepoint more than once – it's just a fact of teenage life for boys in London. It taught them stuff, though – to always keep an eye out, not to have headphones on when walking home late or down a deserted street, to avoid the deserted street in the first place, etc., etc. – and later, they picked up some useful fighting tips from a friend. The difficulty with the young girl who is ogled, or whooped at – or worse – is that this isn't a lesson you want her to learn. Not yet, not in that way, not when she's this young. And the range of unwelcome male advances towards girls is so wide, from catcalling to flashing all the way through to rape.

The Clothing Conversation

Here, we need to have the clothing conversation. Girls see themselves, quite rightly, as being free to wear whatever they like, when they like – a right that their mothers and grandmothers may well have marched in order to support. ('Whatever we wear, wherever we go, yes means yes and no means no!' How loudly we bellowed it.) Very unfortunately, it's not that simple. It doesn't matter that your beautiful fifteen-year-old daughter passionately believes that her clothes are just clothes, that she's chosen to wear them for no reason other than she likes them and feels she looks nice in them, that it is her human right to wear what she chooses. She is dressing like this 'for herself'. But that is not how other people see it, and it is not how predatory boys and men see it. Predatory boys and men think she is dressing like this 'for them'. What to do?

A friend of mine has an unusually beautiful daughter – a world-class beauty, really. People stop and stare at her in the street. Children stop and stare. Dogs stop and stare. She's not, being slightly too young, especially aware of her extraordinary looks. In her mind, she's an ordinary fourteen-year-old. When she goes out with her pod of genuinely ordinary fourteen-year-olds, she doesn't see that people – adults, strangers, men – see her as very distinctly 'other'. This is nice of her: she is not vain, and she doesn't get it (perhaps because she's still at the age when every girl wishes she looked like someone else). All her friends wear cut-off very short shorts, and so does she. They look sweet: some are a bit podgy, with legs that are still sturdy and childlike; some are a bit skinny with knees that are knobbly, like they should be playing on the beach. She has the glossy, toned, perfect legs of a supermodel. And if she's wearing the short shorts, and if she's three steps in front of you on the escalator, you can see the bottom half of her bottom.

When I was a teenager, there was a period when none of my friends wore bras. We had these cut-off, cut-out T-shirts and from the back a bra completely spoiled the look. So nobody wore one. I didn't either. For some reason – wanting to be the same as everyone else, I expect – it didn't occur to me to observe that my friends were all flat-chested. My bra size at the time was 34DD. My mother took one look – I remember exactly where we were: top floor of the house, by the stairs, she on her way to the washing machine with some of my sisters' school uniforms, me on my way out – and she said, 'There is absolutely *no question* of you going out dressed like that.'

Now, if I'd been sensible, I'd have thought this through: my mother was usually cool with whatever I wore, and I wore some fairly out-there things. She wasn't being cool now, though. She looked like a storm in human form. 'Absolutely not,' she repeated. 'Go and get changed.'

I was a virgin, and I was on my way to hang out with girlfriends. She knew both those things. So when I wailed, 'What? But *whyyyyyy*?' she didn't say what my friend also doesn't want to say to her daughter. She couldn't, standing at the top of the stairs, waiting to do the laundry, say to her first-born child, who was *a child*, happy and cheerful and looking forward to an evening with her friends, 'Because someone might rape you.' She couldn't plant that idea in my head: how hideous, how unmaternal, how totally inappropriate. She couldn't say the truth, and this meant that, basically, she couldn't speak. So she did what I described earlier: she turned her fear into anger, raised her voice and shouted at me to get changed this minute, right now. 'For God's sake, why do you always have to be so *difficult?*'

Another friend was braver, recently. It was break-fast on a weekday, and nobody could find anything, and everyone was stressed and going to be late for school, at which point her eldest daughter appeared with her breasts spilling out of her shirt and her school skirt hoiked up to her underwear: a look both glorious and obscene.

'*Nooo*, you can't go out like that,' my friend roared.

'Why?' said the daughter.

'Because you look like a prostitute dressed up as a schoolgirl.'

Her daughter burst into tears.

At this unhappy point my friend burst into tears, too. Because, yes, what a *terrible* thing to say to somebody you love, to your beloved, innocent child: that she looks cheap, vulgar, *like someone who's going out to fuck men for money*, rather than what she is: a child going to school. Poor lovely girl, and poor lovely mum. Blurting out the most appalling words out of protectiveness and terror, really – fearing that something awful should happen to her child – out of love.

There isn't a neat ending or a simple solution, I'm afraid. The daughter didn't readjust her clothes; my friend felt sick all day at what she'd said. However, here is what I think would be a good idea. There is no need to go into the dirty-minded specifics of what might happen, and no need to freak everybody out in the process. But clearly and inexplicably losing your rag out of fear doesn't achieve anything either. So I think there needs to be a rule: 'Wear whatever you like, within reason, but the deal is that you have to take a coat/long top/cardi (season-appropriate) with you, and I trust and love you, so I trust you to wear it.' A couple of years or so later, you can say that with short-shorts comes great responsibility, and explain about the unwelcome male gaze – by which point, sadly, the child is likely to have experienced it at first hand, and to concur with most of what you're saying.

Mother–Daughter Competition

This seems as good a place as any to mention those women who are competitive with their own daughters as those daughters blossom into womanhood;[3]

---

[3] Yuck, I can't believe I said 'blossom into womanhood'.

where it happens, it often starts at around the problematic clothing stage of teenagehood. I want to throw those women in the bin, so I don't expect I'm about to say anything very measured here, but really – please don't do this. It is so awful, and so bewildering to your daughter, and so fucked-up and weird, and so unattractive.

You are her mother, who has loved and nurtured her all her life, and now suddenly – inexplicably – you have reinvented yourself as her competition. I mean, it would turn a person mad, that kind of behaviour: like *Single White Female*, except to your own child. Just: no. You've had your teenagehood and your youth, and it's gone. Pretending it hasn't is horrendously embarrassing for everyone concerned, and chiefly for you. Don't ape your daughter's slang, don't plonk yourself down among her friends just as they're hunkering down with a box set and pizza, don't flirt with any boys she might ask to tea, don't change your wardrobe, don't – please – take her shopping and end up buying the same clothes. Don't share a wardrobe. Don't gang up with her against her dad (who will be absolutely appalled at the sight of his wife being competitive with his daughter and will wonder whether you're having an especially difficult menopause).[4]

---

[4] Let me quote the brilliant Tracey Thorn's brilliant song 'Hormones' here: 'And I have to own up / That dress looks better on you now / Only half grown up / You should really twirl, take a bow / You ask me what's going on /

Be delighted, instead. You have produced this gorgeous creature through a combination of genes (yours! Well done!) and upbringing (yours! Bravo!). Delight in her loveliness, in her smooth brow, in her peachy skin and shiny hair, just as you delighted in her baby smell and her fat little legs.

Please don't be jealous of your own child – it is just the utter pits.

THE ROLE OF THE MODERN STEPMOTHER

Fairy tales have a lot to answer for. There's nothing society fears more than a woman of a certain age who is still, clearly, having sex. Fairy tales are never shy about reminding us. Now imagine that woman, and imagine she's shagging your dad. And you're twelve.

Now stop imagining anything, and just look in the mirror: that woman is you. It is not necessarily *ideal*.

But nor is it necessarily a disaster.

The main thing to remember about being a step-parent is that the best you can hope for is to be thought of fondly, either at the time (ideal) or in retrospect (not bad). Everything else is cherries on cakes. The exact same thing is true of you as

---

Why do we feel this way? / I can only shake my head / "Hormones, babe" I say / And yours are just kicking in / And mine are just checking out.'

stepchild. Viewed with fondness: winning. Anything else: bonus. But since I'm not writing a book for stepchildren, we'll focus on the you-as-step-parent scenario. NB: I am assuming here that you are the stepmother to a child (or children) who has two living parents, i.e. that nobody is widowed and that no one has died. If someone *has* died, go back a bit and read the sections on parenting, because that's now what you are.

Here is the thing with step-parenting: there's no way of getting it 100 per cent right. But there isn't a way of getting normal, biological parenting 100 per cent right, either. So cut yourself some slack, and now cut yourself some more. Remember, too, that this isn't something you signed up to. You fell in love with someone who happened to have children, and now here you all are. How you feel about those children largely depends on how immediately likeable they are to you, which may be anything from 'hugely' to 'not a lot'. It is not a terrible failure to struggle to be charmed by utterly uncharming, hostile and/or mutinous children (and see the box on page 133). Sad but true, and something your partner needs to understand (I'll get to the opposite situation – your kids, not his – in a bit).

Having said that, *they're children*. It's hard for them, even though it needn't be (i.e. it's possibly made harder by outside factors that they, being children, have little or no control over). An enormous amount of what happens next depends on the kind of relationship – actively friendly, amicable, frosty, wary, hostile – that your partner has with his ex. I can't emphasize this enough: it is wholly, *wholly* to your advantage to encourage him to have the best possible relationship with her. If you're the kind of person who says, 'God, why is your ex-wife being such a total bitch?' when she's done or said something that is mildly irritating and, frankly, no skin off your nose whatsoever, you are creating the mightiest rod for your own back. It is not generally necessary to discuss people's ex-wives with them other than in the most general – and, crucially, benign – terms.

NB: This also applies if said ex-wife is not general or benign about you, but instead specific and malevolent. It doesn't matter. She is not in your lives; the malevolence is a clunky attempt at shoe-horning herself in, because angry attention is better than no attention. If she wants to mutter darkly from the sidelines, it's a shame, but what can you do, other than let her? Somebody has to be grand and behave well, in these situations, and it may as well be you. Even if it doesn't change anything, at least you're not down in the mud, wrestling.

I am strongly in favour of the full charm offensive, when it comes to the mother of your partner's children: a) you have something in common, though you may choose not to point this out while snorting with laughter, and b) he fell for her. On the basis that he also fell for you and that he doesn't have dementedly horrendous taste, she must be OK. At least, this is broadly true. Everyone has a proper, full-on horror in their cupboard somewhere, but they're not usually the ones they have children with.

Getting to Know Your Stepchildren

Now, the actual stepchildren. There are two crucial things to remember:

* **They will have, now and for evermore, absolute, cast-iron, unshakeable loyalty to their mother.** This is right, and correct, and exactly as it should be. You will know this if you are already a parent yourself. If you aren't, do please pay attention to this next bit, because it is very important. If you try to shake that loyalty, if you try to bend or undermine or shift it towards you, you will be doing a terrible thing, and the terrible thing will have terrible, unhappy repercussions, mostly for you. That's point one. Don't go there. They already have a mum. They don't need or want another one. It's not a competition – and even if it were, it would be one you could never win.

* **Divorce or separation do not break a family or cause it to somehow stop existing.** They merely displace it and make it geographically disparate. The family still exists, just in a

different way. Assuming no one's died, children have two parents. Nothing can change that – and you are not one of those parents.

What does that mean practically? Well, it means that if you are mean, needy or selfish enough to try replacing the children's mother in their affections, they will eventually hate you for it. Children liking you slightly more than they like their mother does their heads in. It is a great unkindness to even try.

NB: Sometimes the children *like* you to try, because they are charmed or amused by you, annoyed with their own mum that particular weekend, or whatever. 'Why, these children adore me,' you will think to yourself delightedly. The trouble is, sooner or later they will feel guilty about liking you so much (they're absolutely fine, and generally guiltless, about *quite* liking you). You need to make it as easy as possible for them to suddenly fall back again to a default position of liking you well enough, without feeling hurt that they apparently liked you even more last time they visited. That means not sulking, not wheedling, 'What's wrong, guys?' (ugh), not moaning to their father that the graph of their affections zigzags up and down in a really unpredictable way. The zigzags are completely normal. Just take them in your stride, and don't take them personally.

As a child, you want a stepmother – or stepfather,

for that matter – to be benign and reassuring, but *not too great*. As a step-parent, what you should aim for is friendship. Depending on their ages, and yours, that can be anything from a sort of nice auntie to an older sister relationship (without older sister teasing, preferably – and I mean this. Teasing is a manifestation of great intimacy and can strike even sweet-tempered people as unpleasantly overfamiliar. Careful who you tease).

Also, know when to stand back. Don't always insert yourself into anecdotes, for example. If they are all chatting about the time they went camping, and you know about it because your partner's told you the story, don't butt in with, 'And then the cow chased Daddy round the field, didn't it? Hahahaha!' It's their story, about their time together, and it's their cherished memory – leave them to own it. Equally, if you don't know the story, don't try to trump it with a better, funnier cow 'n' camping story of your own. You exist, uninvited, in their present life. There's no need to insist on colonizing their past, too.

Some more words of caution about specific situations:

* **Don't do The Look.** I can't believe how many people do The Look, as if the other people present were actually blind. The Look is when a child says something like, 'Mummy says vaccinations are dangerous.' You know that you need to bite your tongue in these sorts of

situations, rather than diss the child's mother for her arse-headed stupidity, so you say nothing, but you do The Look instead, locking eyes with your partner for slightly too long. For some reason that I can't fathom at all, adults think The Look is subtle and discreet. It never is. Everyone notices. You may as well have yelled, 'Oh my God, is your mum an actual fuckwit, or what?' Same effect. Don't do The Look.

* **Never, ever volunteer an opinion on sartorial issues** – unless specifically called upon to do so by the child or children. This includes in the middle of their dad having a row with the kids over an item of clothing, with him saying to you, 'Help me out here.' Don't take sides with him – it will make the children feel ganged up on. If you absolutely have to say something, try to keep it non-committal.

* **If you feel strongly that the children are right, it's fine to gently say so,** in general argument situations. But don't say so just to make them happy, in any circumstances. They can tell the difference.

* **Never volunteer an opinion on weight or physical appearance.** You may think it's helpful to say, 'I got you some spot cream,' because when you say it to your own children

they say, 'Oh cool, cheers,' and then they don't have spots any more: result. That isn't always the case with children who may be appallingly self-conscious, generally less breezy, and away from home to boot. Equally – and I shouldn't really have to point this out – never say 'Really?' when a podgy child asks for seconds or says she's excited about pudding. Ditto remarks such as, 'You could do with a run around,' and so on. When in doubt, just imagine how you'd feel if someone said it to you.

Having advocated caution in certain areas, I think it's fine – desirable, even – not to adjust your behaviour in other respects. These children are human beings, not pieces of china, and they'll have a far better, and more honest, relationship with you if you behave like the person you are. If you're not lovely all the time – and who is? – let your unloveliness show every now and then.

It is also perfectly possible to let them know you're displeased without going into agonies about it: just tell them off normally (i.e. not like a socio-path who's stored up a whole load of grievances and is letting them all out in one big, dispropor-tionate flood). If they're rude, or completely unresponsive, or apparently profoundly ungrateful, it's fine to say something.

This last – ingratitude – is a classic: the father gives the child an unusually nice, longed-for present; the child appears unusually unenthusiastic about it. It's because the child knows, at some instinctive level, that the parent may be trying – perhaps subconsciously – to atone for being absent from their day-to-day life. The child's apparent lack of enthusiasm is a way of saying, 'You don't excuse your absence that easily.' Of course, nobody's trying to excuse anything, or to buy love – but as the child in this situation, that's often how you feel, regardless. At the end of the weekend, the child goes home and is free to express delirious joy at the present. Hurrah!

Helping Your Children Adjust to a New Stepmother

Now, some advice for the actual mother – I mean, the mother who's sent her children away for the weekend to spend time with their dad and his new wife/partner:

1. **Never refer, even jokingly, to the dad's 'new family'.** At the very best you will sound pathetically defensive and in need of reassurance. It is not your children's job to find you pathetic or to reassure you.[5] And you'll be planting an idea in their head that may not have existed if you hadn't articulated it. Plus, as I was saying on page 157, there's no such thing as a 'new family'. It's an extension of

[5] Ever, in any context.

your children's existing family, nothing more – and being an extension, it very much includes them.

2. **Use people's names and use them respectfully.** Unflattering nicknames and terms like 'fancy woman', 'her' and 'whatsit' don't reflect well on you. Like, at all.

3. **Don't belittle their father's choices.** So you may not like his new wife. So what? Whether you like her or not is irrelevant. What is relevant is trying to make sure that she has a good relationship with your children, because they will be spending time with her now. It's hard for her to even start doing that if she sees the children as living extensions of your anger, disdain or rancour, or if they come up with snarky little phrases they could only conceivably have learned from you.

4. **Don't belittle their father.** You eagerly married him, after all, so aside from anything else, it's not making you sound too clever. Also, if you lie to children, they will find you out. Don't say he's awful and selfish if he's lovely and generous *to them*: as they get older, your children will eventually start aggressively questioning your judgement. All children want to love both parents. Don't make it hard for them. Your children know that half of

them is their dad. How do you expect them to cope with the idea that that immutable half is disgusting?

5. **You will form an instant opinion of your ex's partner,** whether you've met her once or thirty or three hundred times. Keep that opinion to yourself, unless it is wholly and cheerfully positive, or unless you can spin it to be so when you voice it out loud. Do bear in mind that she will also have formed an instant opinion of *you*.

6. **If your children come back from a day, weekend or holiday having had a lovely time, be delighted.** Never make your kids feel bad for having a nice time. Know (see page 157) that their primary loyalty is to you, and that they may already be feeling guilty for having had fun – as if having fun were disloyal to you.

7. **Be pleased that they feel safe and secure with the stepmother.** Yes, their occasional unbridled enthusiasm may make you feel sad or even displaced or cast aside. But you must remember that the situation is not their fault.

8. **You are the adult.** This is really the most crucial thing of all. Never put your children in a position where *they* are having to parent *you*. It is not their job to feel that they must

164

tamp down their enthusiasm (in which case you've made them lie to you, by this point: they have learned to lie to spare your feelings. That's fucked up).

9. **You won't like everything about the way in which your ex and his partner do things** – just as, no doubt, they don't like everything about the way you do things. Suck it up, in both cases.

Despite my advice in point 9, what do you do if your children are *really* not keen on their stepmother?

1. **If she's childless herself, it's a very steep learning curve.** Think of what you might be able to do to help.

2. **If she has a new baby – well, you know how exhausting new babies can be.** Don't be furious that she isn't devoting every second of the day to her stepchildren. If this is the situation, and if things are fraught, it may be kinder to everybody to turn the weekend visits into single days until, say, the baby is sleeping through the night.

3. **Ask yourself: why don't they like her?** Do they not like her because she's dislikeable? Or do they not like her because she's 'taken' their

dad 'away'? Or do they not like her because of their loyalty to you? These are three different things. The second and third options you can do a lot about, by sitting them down and having a chat. This chat may not gladden your heart – but again, this is about your children's relationships, not about yours.

4. **Don't feel shy about speaking to your ex (calmly),** if his new partner is straightfor-wardly dislikeable or, worse, unkind. I do actually know someone to whom this happened – awkward, but the children were right. I can't emphasize enough that in this scenario, or in any scenario involving awkwardness, the better and healthier the relationship with your ex, the better and easier it is to resolve problems.

5. **Is she benignly neglectful?** This can happen if she is, for instance, much younger and more interested in having a fun time than in looking after grumpy teenagers who aren't even hers. Well, it's a bit annoying, but it does no harm. It's a weekend, not an adoption try-out.

As a footnote to the above advice, remember that divorce and separation are also a real bummer for the children's grandparents – it's hardly their fault, either. Try to maintain good relationships here too, so that your children sometimes see their paternal grandparents – and other relatives – with you, rather than just with their dad. This usually means that the grandparents get double the sightings, which is much nicer for them.

Helping Your Children Adjust to a New Stepfather

Right, so now what if you're the one with kids, and a man – possibly a man with children – comes into all your lives?

* **Only introduce him to your children when you know you have something serious going on** (always make him aware that the children exist, though, from the off). Introducing people, encouraging a degree of emotional involvement from all parties, and then things not working out and the children never seeing him again is just confusing – and a bit sad and upsetting. So never introduce anyone to your children of whom you're 'not sure'.

* **This means initially having dates when the house is empty** – either when the children are at their dad's, say, or when you can get a babysitter and stay over at his.

* **Once you think the relationship has legs, introduce the children to the new partner as soon as possible.** This is because it is deeply weird for children to know or suspect that you

have a secret life away from them with, as they see it, a stranger. What if the stranger is an axe murderer? Also, once children know of the existence of the new partner, if you leave it too long they will spend time feeling anxious about meeting him. What if he doesn't like them? What if he seems mean? And so on. Knock that on the head asap.

* **Make it clear from the outset that all you expect is kindness and civility from both sides.** There is no need whatsoever to try to force anything more than that. If and when your children and new partner become close, then marvellous. But it needs to be organic, not artificial.

* **Never, ever ask your children to call a man who isn't their father 'Daddy',** even if you are widowed. They may eventually suggest it themselves, if they are very small. This is because all children are innately deeply conservative and want to live in a house with a mummy and a daddy in it. It's up to you, of course, but I would discourage it on grounds of respect (and complications later on – 'He's not actually my daddy,' and so on). If your partner's name feels too cold and unfriendly, you can suggest they come up with a nickname instead. Would you like your kids to call your ex's new partner 'Mummy'?

* **If everyone gets on like a house on fire, great.** But bear in mind that if he has children of his own, those children may initially find his intimacy with *your* children startling when they come to stay. Or they may not. But keep an eye out – sometimes that situation needs managing, which is easily done by suggesting that your partner and his own children go off and do things together. Nobody has to play the Waltons every minute of every day: not every outing has to be communal; and children having time alone with their parent is very important.

* **However, I am heavily pro-Waltons in general.** Lump 'em all together, make a big ol' load of nice food and have a big ol' lunch, that's what I say. One can overthink these things and tie oneself up in knots, and I do think that when presented with a new situation, it's always best just to crack on cheerfully. This is real life, after all, not some sort of cautious, anxiety-filled rehearsal for it. You only get nervous about things if you stand around speculating. Jump straight in, and those nerves don't even have a chance to get started.

* **Finally: what if nobody gets on, at all, even after months or years?** This is crucial: never choose the man over the children. Equally, never tell the children that you've chosen them

over the man (mother-as-martyr is the weakest and probably most problematic of looks. We're not in Holy Catholic Ireland in 1950).

Have a different sort of relationship with your partner: less domestic and more based on dates outside the house. Personally, I wouldn't fancy it, or not for long, but your mileage may vary. There are only two probable causes here: a) your children are insecure and very, very difficult (fixable, eventually) or b) the man isn't making enough of an effort with them (hopeless but understandable, though, if they are a total ball-ache). If nobody gets on and you're all living together, you can try to compartmentalize up to a point, but it's really almost impossible. Personally, I could never be with a man who disliked my children.

WHEN A PARENT REMARRIES WHEN YOU ARE AN ADULT

By 'an adult', I don't mean that you're twenty-one but rather in middle age or beyond yourself, which depending on your circumstances might make your newly wed parent really pretty old. People are always terribly startled when old people remarry, especially when they remarry after bereavement with what looks like unseemly haste. Here's the thing: people who were happily married for thirty years really *like* being happily married, and by extension don't like being widowed and single. If somebody personable comes along and suggests a union, it's hard to see why they would say no. They know that it won't be 'the same', but they are elastic and broad-minded enough to go cheerfully into a relationship that will provide them with a companion to share their days with.

Of course this can be deeply shocking to the person's adult children – aside from anything else, it seems so disrespectful to their late parent. But think about it calmly: why should your mum or dad, a person who may have been defined by their marriage, willingly choose to end his or her days alone? Do you think they have some sort of duty to suffer for evermore or to resign themselves to their unhappy lot? Of course not. Once you've ascertained that the proposed bride/groom is a decent person and not some sort of terrible eighty-something gigolo/scarlet woman on the make (unlikely, to be honest, though not impossible), the best thing you can do is be happy for your parent. If you can't manage that, pretend to be happy. The saddest thing you can do is withdraw your approval, thereby making your beloved parent (recently bereaved) deeply miserable and feeling like they are being forced to choose between their own personal happiness and their children's blessing.

There are usually four main areas of concern:

- **You may not love your new step-parent's adult children.**

- **You may feel jealous if your parent seems to adore them.**

- **You may be suspicious of them.**

- **You may worry that you will have to share your inheritance with them.**

Unless anything obviously sinister is afoot, suck it up. Do not create drama around old people getting together, just be glad that they have.

CHAPTER 5

HEALTH AND SENSE

What to do about bodily decrepitude,
and how to party

Bodily *decrepitude is wisdom*, W. B. Yeats wrote.[1] Ol' William Butler clearly never slid on a pavement and hurt his Achilles tendon to the point where he was forced to hobble around for weeks in quasi-permanent agony, cursing the very concept of decrepitude and wondering whether he would ever heal. Because that's the thing about health in one's Prime: it used to be that something would go wrong, and you'd think, 'Ouch! I've bashed my knee,' and then you'd forget about it and just wait for it to heal. Which it would, within days, and off you would gaily skip with nary a backward glance.

Those days are over, unfortunately. Ailments linger. You wait for your twisted ankle to get better, and find it never quite goes back to being exactly how it was. Things start happening to your back.

[1] It's from 'After Long Silence': 'Bodily decrepitude is wisdom; young / We loved each other and were ignorant.'

'I think I put my back out,' you say, with a look of pure disbelief on your face because, really – what, are you ninety-two now? Even sleeping isn't safe – twice this year I've cricked my neck in my sleep.

BE VIGILANT

First piece of advice: if something bothers you for more than two days, GO TO THE DOCTOR. It won't just 'go away eventually' – not at our age.

Feet

I refer you back crucially to the need for constant FOOT VIGILANCE – I could repeat myself here, such is the importance of FV, but instead see page 15.

Legs

Leg vigilance is important, too. You don't want to be of a certain age and have those sad legs that are all bruised and marked. Your ankles may be weedier too; mine certainly are, but that's possibly because I broke one when I was young. Be really careful wearing heels in bad weather, because you can no longer recover from the icy-ground pratfall as springily or as effectively as you think – and this applies even if you're the heel queen who's worn stilettoes since she was thirteen. It's a very good idea to have some sort of sensible footwear (yeesh) about your person, if not actually permanently on your feet (like hooves), when you know you're going to have to walk in the sheeting rain/snow. Keep a pair of something grippy in your bag/desk drawer and change into them when you go outside: not glamorous, but a great deal more glamorous than having a debilitating old-lady injury at the age of forty-five.

NB: Sensible footwear doesn't just mean 'comfortable' – it means 'properly fitted' and 'with grip'. Shoes that are comfortable without being properly fitted make your feet go weird and spready and your toes go all clenched.[2] DO try not to fall over: take all possible precautions. From about fifty upwards, you don't necessarily fully recover. (The other awful thing about falls – but that comes later – is that in the very old they don't necessarily result from, say, falling off a stepladder. They can happen because bones or joints just give out of their own accord, because they're weak and worn out[3]).

---

[2] In my view, in really dire weather you can't do better than Sorel boots (sorelfootwear.co.uk), which I personally find attractive as well as effective.

[3] In the context of ailing parents, you can request a home-hazard assessment, designed to identify things that are likely to cause falls/slips, either via their GP or through their local authority (see gov.uk).

Knees

I know this is a really annoying thing to say, especially if you're a committed runner of twenty years' standing, but I am at the age (forty-eight) when *all* my running friends no longer run because they've absolutely ruined their knees, which are straightforwardly worn out. It's just the way knees are built, with a finite amount of spongy stuff in the middle that gets knackered and doesn't regenerate. Now, if you're a runner you'll know about how best to avoid this, and I'm not a sports therapist: seek a second and third opinion about whether running is damaging to knees. My evidence is only anecdotal – though there's plenty of it – but my advice is AVOID. Of course it's not just running that knackers your knees: if you're very overweight that buggers them up, too. And of course you wouldn't be as overweight if you went running. But there are so many other forms of exercise that we know are safe – swimming, for one (at our age, buoyancy is our friend) – that I'd go for one of those instead.

NB: You can also knacker your knees on cross-trainers. Poor knees: NOWHERE IS SAFE. I don't want to sound like a broken record, but: do yoga.

Thighs

Having done feet and legs, I should mention thighs. Here's the salient fact: there is nothing you can do about cellulite. Not a single one of those creams or treatments works effectively enough to make a discernable difference. I hate those products: they pick on a particularly acute insecurity and foster false hope. Forget them. The really good things about cellulite are a) everyone has it, to some extent, even 23-year-old models, and b) you can't see it because it's behind you. Given that c) there is literally nothing you can do about it, it doesn't seem to me to be something to be wasting time over. Also d), I so ardently hope you and I are *too old* to fret about this kind of neurotic wankery. **One of the really important things about ageing happily and successfully is developing the ability to go 'fuck it'.** Be pleased that your legs work, cellulitey or not, and get on with your life.

Whack some fake tan on your legs instead – that always helps. For my money, the best fake tan currently on the market is Elemis Total Glow Bronzing Body Lotion. It not only gives a really nice, convincing (gradual) colour regardless of whether you're olive-skinned or the colour of milk, but it's hard to mess up. In an emergency – of the 'I must have tanned legs right this second but I'm scared of it going wrong' variety – there exist excellent temporary fake tans that wash off. Of these, my favourite is One Night Tanned by Soap and Glory (excellent brand, despite the youthful playfulness of its branding – they also do an excellent cleanser called The Ultimelt).

Hands

Watch your hands, as well. I was recently crippled by pain in my right hand. I thought it might be RSI but it turned out to be something unattractively and rather belittlingly called Washerwoman's Hand, aka BlackBerry Thumb – except that I have a washing machine and an iPhone. It's also known as De Quervain's tenosynovitis. Anyway, you get it from being on your phone too much and, in my case, from earning your living by typing – which, given how much time we all spend at a keyboard, regardless of profession, means that we're all at risk.

The pain started shooting up my arm, and then into my shoulder, and got so bad that it stopped me sleeping. Because I am an idiot, I didn't go to the doctor until I had giant black shadows under my eyes: I kept thinking that it would pass, or that it was symptomatic of something deeply sinister that I'd rather not know about. So then I had to go and have *un*believably painful steroid injections, which helped a bit. (My hand is actually feeling rather sore as I type, but that's probably psychosomatic.) What would have helped more would have been to have a proper desk instead of the kitchen table, a proper ergonomic chair, and to type properly, i.e. with the wrists at the correct angle. In brief:

* **The chair should allow you to change its height, back position and tilt;** you should

adjust it so that your lower back is properly supported.

* **Your knees should be level with your hips.**

* **Your computer screen should be at eye level.**

* **When using the keyboard,** your wrists and forearms should be straight and parallel with the floor. Your feet should be flat on the floor, not crossed at the ankle.

If you're reading this and frequently type in a bad position or at the wrong angle/gradient, get yourself organized right now – you may have been lucky so far, but the luck runs out. Spend the money on one of those ugly ergonomic chairs. It is so worth it. Two of my writer friends now type while wearing special splints, and it's a permanent rather than a temporary solution. This is not hot.

Stomach

Moving on up, skirting coyly past The Area (because it gets its moment in the spotlight in chapter 9), we get to the stomach. I cannot bring good news here, only empathy. It is an unbelievably irritating fact that, for the majority of women, a thickening middle is an eventual inevitability

– rounder stomach, thicker waist. I'm always reminded of tubby insects and of insect parts – abdomen, thorax – combining to give a bee-like shape to the middle of the body. In my wilder moments I sometimes think this is nature's way of altering your centre of gravity, so that you are more grounded and less likely to fall over. Most of the time, though, I just find this thickening really quite annoying: no wonder women go mad and decide they're huge and live in elasticated trousers/smocks.

Here's the thing, though: nobody other than you notices. I know this because all my female friends bemoan their newly thickened middles, and I am very beady and observant and I truly haven't noticed – not even on the beach. You're not really huge, and there's no need for the elastic. Also, I personally like a convex stomach, within reason – or at least I don't think it's disastrous. It's friendly. As I keep saying, a little convexity here and there gives the impression of lushness; a concave body gives the impression of ungenerosity.

Bosom

Movin' on up: tits. The thing about tits is that no two pairs are alike, ever – even in teenagehood – so there's no need to feel self-conscious about yours: it's not like there's a sort of tit norm to adhere to (unless you've had cosmetic surgery). I don't think anyone should moan about their tits, and I will brook no dissent. I *love* mine, actually. Not because they're so fantastically great, but because there are two of them, intact (I can't tell you how many people I know who've had breast cancer); because they look nice when I'm naked (they're a bore in clothes, being Not Small, but I'm used to that by now); and because – well, you know, no complaints.

I think that at this age you're only really allowed to dislike one body part, otherwise you sound neurotic and a bit mad and teenager-angsting-in-the-bedroom. I don't like my stomach (size 16 and three C-sections). Everything else is fine. Because that's the point, isn't it? It doesn't have to be incredible, just fine. So if you have big tits: rejoice. Nobody doesn't like big tits – apart from their owners, if their owners don't have good underwear. If you have flat tits, or no tits: rejoice. You will never look matronly, you can wear all the clothes *and* the cosy polo necks, and you can play beach volleyball without looking pornographic, which I imagine must be a nice feeling.

DRESSING THE LARGER BOSOM

Bottom line: this used to be hard when you were twenty-five, but now it's easy. You used to have to go to specialist shops, like Bravissimo (still great, though) or Rigby & Peller (ditto). Now you can go online, or to any department store, to kit yourself out. Some ranges go up to a J or a K cup, somewhat incredibly: you should be fine. There is absolutely no need to wear a bra that doesn't fit *perfectly* any more, and if you're not doing this already, I strongly urge you – command you, actually – to go and do it AT ONCE because the effect of a good bra is figure-altering.

So. Lecture over. I'm just saying, don't be one of those older women who gets that sort of awful slope, where the bosoms meld into the stomach, giving a Weeble effect. There is no need whatsoever for this to happen; it's really doing yourself a major disservice.

Neck and Jowls

Crêpey cleavage and chicken-neck (easy, Tiger): see page 45.

As for jowls, these happen – and as if the drooping weren't bad enough, they make their owner look permanently disapproving. As with so many things to do with ageing, they can be exacerbated by sudden weight loss, so I repeat to you my mantra: **don't be too fat, and don't be too thin**. Jowls can be helped along enormously by filler injected into the line of droop, but they cannot – as far as I am aware – be eradicated fully without going under the knife.

Chin

Chins can double (or triple), and jawlines can sag and lose definition. Diet may help solve the former, but there's not a lot you can do about the latter. The worst thing – or perhaps *a* worst thing – about chins is the sudden sprouting of individual hair (your oestrogen and progesterone levels are dropping, but your testosterone is either remaining static or rising. Rising = more hair, but also better sex. Every cloud). This is made extra bizarre by the fact that the hair appears not to grow at the normal rate but springs forth fully formed, often measuring whole centimetres. Chin and Upper Lip Vigilance must join Foot Vigilance.

Hair Removal

Never travel without a really good pair of tweezers about you; I still swear by the Tweezerman brand, which extract precisely and effortlessly where lesser tweezers just poke ineffectually.

Regarding actual hair removal, you may find that the old Jolen Creme Bleach no longer cuts it, if you're dark – it just turns the hair yellow (which, as I wrote in my book *The Shops*, gives you a Dutch-porn-star moustache rather than a Frida Kahlo: not necessarily a vast improvement).

* **Solution number 1: hair-removal cream**
  – a product whose straightforward efficacy

has been overshadowed by lasers, IPL, waxing, threading, and so on. You need a face-specific cream, because you'll damage your skin if you just whack on leg removal cream, which is too strong. The best one I have found is made by Avon and is called Skin So Soft (Fresh & Smooth). Unfortunately, it doesn't seem to be available from Avon UK, but you can buy it online from other outlets, and inexpensively. Whether you use this or a more easily sourced brand, wear loads of sunblock afterwards, if it's sunny, otherwise you may get dark marks.[4]

* **Solution number 2: a little gadget called the Tweezy** – basically a very tightly wound wire coil, in a stick shape, that you bend into a U shape. By twisting the handles at the base of the coil, you make the Tweezy roll across whatever facial surface, yanking hair out by the root as it does so. I'm making it sound much more complicated than it is – in fact you don't

---

[4] You should be wearing this every day anyway; sun damage is the pits. You want something thin and non-greasy that's not going to leave claggy white marks everywhere, or block your pores and make your skin feel caked. I like Bioderma's Photoderm Max range. They also do a brilliant one called Photoderm Laser, which is specifically for people with either existing dark patches or people with highly sensitized skin (e.g. following laser treatment).

need any skill or even a mirror. Not painless, but cheap and effective.[5]

* **Solution number 3: threading and waxing,** both of which work beautifully if you can hack them – I can't and develop huge, red welts (I'm fine with eyebrows. Weird).

* **Solution number 4: lasering and IPL (intense pulsed light) treatment,** which zaps hair to death, never to return (eventually). Find a reputable practitioner or have a look at the very expensive but very good home version by Philips, called Lumea, which you can use on the face as well as on underarms, bikini line, and so on.

    NB: It used to be that this method was unsuitable for darker skins; that is no longer the case, but always do a patch test first.

Mouths

Marionette lines – two verticals from the corners of your mouth, heading down – happen to everyone, so let's not over-fret. However, they can happen really quite dramatically, giving the effect – like with jowls, but worse – that you are terribly disappointed and sad and that life has dealt you a series of low blows. They're also very ageing.

[5] £10 from victoriahealth.com.

Here I am an enthusiastic and unapologetic fan of Botox (in the corners of the mouth, for a very, very slight lifting effect. The lines remain – you need filler for that – but the mouth looks cheerful).

Noses and Earlobes

These keep growing. Hurrah! Personally there is nothing I love more than a proper nose, on a man or on a woman – I don't think faces look like faces unless they have a *strong* nose sitting in the middle. But if your nose is growing into a beak, like on those Venetian masks, there are surgical steps you can take. The Buddha-like earlobes are more of an acquired taste, but ditto.

Teeth

It's time to develop a close relationship with your dentist in middle age. As I will never tire of repeating, NOTHING IS AS AGEING AS AWFUL TEETH. Happily, dentistry is amazing and can perform all sorts of tooth miracles (including dental implants. Remember how old people used to have either dentures or just missing teeth? No need. Implants. Unless you've smoked so much that your bone density is too weedy).

My most recent dental lesson – aside from not smoking (more about that in a second) – is the supreme excellence of those little interdental brushes. I used to spend my time flossing, but your teeth move around as you get older, and you acquire gaps that are wider than the width of floss – even fat floss (I love fat floss). Enter the brushes: and they are the business (they are also disgustingly satisfying to use). If you're constantly getting food stuck in, or between, particular teeth, these are your guys. Ask your dentist, or go to a big chemist. A really good brand is Dent-O-Care. You might want to brush-floss after every meal. It's slightly obsessive, but there's nothing wrong with banishing plaque before it even has the time to *form*.

THE PERILS OF SMOKING IN YOUR PRIME

I've always had reasonably decent teeth despite smoking from the age of thirteen (a bit) to forty-eight (a lot). Smoking is absolutely **the worst thing** you can do to your mouth (and the rest), as various dentists and hygienists have never tired of telling me, over several decades. But the thing is, you either smoke or you don't. And if you do, you make a polite, interested face and say, 'Oh really? Fascinating,' while internally going, 'YADA YADA YADA, TELL IT TO THE MARINES.' But anyway, my teeth were fine, due to bleaching trays, my trusty Sonicare toothbrush and frequent (monthly) visits to the hygienist.

And then – the horror – one day my gums, which

I had meanwhile observed were not as perky-looking as they might be, went to pot. I was sitting there in the chair, and the hygienist said that I had gum disease. Lots of people get gum disease, but smokers don't get the warning signs – bleeding – because their gums are all seized up as a result of reduced blood flow from smoking. What eventually happens is you get periodontal disease, where bone density is lost – that's the bone attaching your teeth to your jaw – and your teeth start falling out. It's really gross.

Well, who wants that? I was walking around with the possibility of this tooth catastrophe in my head – because that's how smoking works: you push aside the terrible, fatal things that might happen and fixate on a lesser thing (and I am obsessed with teeth) – and then one day I was on Facebook and asked, idly and with no real intention of following anything through, whether anyone I knew had tried vaping, or e-cigarettes. I got such a fulsome and glowing report back from someone I trusted – and whose smoking was an addiction, rather than something they did at parties – that I took the plunge; it is now six months since I smoked a cigarette. It has been entirely, 100 per cent painless, and it makes me feel happy every day. I smell really nice, my lung capacity appears to have increased one thousand-fold, I've got more money and, unexpectedly, much more energy. Here's what you need to know.

HOW TO VAPE

NB: The jury's currently out on whether vaping is straightforwardly magical or still not especially good for you. The way I see it is this: tobacco smoke contains nicotine (addictive, but that's it) and 4,000 chemicals, of which seventy are *known carcinogens*. These include tar, arsenic, formaldehyde and polonium. When you vape, you are inhaling nicotine and a vegetable-based flavouring – none of those cancer-causing chemicals, and no poisons. And yes, the nicotine is still addictive, obviously. The point is, you don't die of nicotine addiction (you don't die from nicotine patches, for instance), you die from the other stuff. So the choice is yours. I have never been able to stop smoking before, and now I don't smoke. If you're reading this bit, you are presumably a smoker who loves smoking but not the consequences of smoking – a regretful addict. Right? Me, too. Read on:

- **Vaping is utterly satisfying.** It is not 'almost' as satisfying as smoking – it is *as* satisfying; long-term devotees would say it is better, because you can regulate the size and strength of the hit depending on your mood. As a friend, also a convert to vaping, put it: 'I can't believe how *old-fashioned* smoking seems now.'

- **You get an identical hit to the back of the throat from a vape as you do from a smoke** – and see above: you can adjust it, too.
- **Tobacco tastes kind of disgusting.** With vaping, you can have whatever flavour you like. If you don't think tobacco tastes disgusting, you can have that too – really *good* tobacco. One brand even steeps it in old sherry or bourbon casks.
- **If you have a sweet tooth, you'll be in heaven.** You can vape Jaffa Cakes, if you like. Vanilla custard. Liquorice Allsorts, Jelly Babies, cake. I find those a bit much, having a salty tooth. But, you know – there's a flavour out there for absolutely every taste. My current fixation is a flavour called Venus in Vapes[6] – all this, and a Velvet Underground reference! – which tastes of aniseed, molasses, vanilla custard and apple purée. Yep.
- **The kit:** you need a battery, a tank to hold the liquid (this is called a clear-omizer) and some e-liquid (this is

[6] The make is Halcyon Haze, from halcyonhaze.co.uk.

called juice. Vaping vocab does leave a little to be desired). The very best way of getting all this stuff is to get yourself to a vaping shop, where someone will explain it all properly, and where you can sit down and try a zillion different flavours and strengths before buying.

- **If you can't visit a shop, go online.** All the sites sell starter kits for about £20, and then you buy the juice on top. My recommendation – there's a *lot* of vaping kit out there, and it can get a bit overwhelming – is to go for an eGo-type battery and a tank (clearomizer) that's made out of Pyrex, because I don't like the idea of inhaling from plastic. Pyrex tanks cost marginally more, but not much.

- **You want me to recommend a specific kit, don't you?** OK, but bear in mind that the techy components of vaping move very fast, and that my recommendation may have been improved/renamed by the time this book comes out. I started with a crappy kit to see what I made of vaping, but very quickly went out and bought a kit by Innokin called iTaste CLK. It had everything I needed except the juice, and cost £30.[7] I then bought a Pyrex tank for an extra £15. I'm still using this exact equipment.

- **You can decrease the nicotine content of your juice as the weeks go by,** until the point where you're nicotine-free. You can then pack the whole thing in, if that's your wish.
- **Those crappy e-cigs you get from the newsagent are nonsense and don't work,** as should be clear from the above.
- **The bummer:** you'd think that your gums would do a dance of joy when you stop smoking. Not so: it gets worse before it gets better. They bleed like mad at first, and you may also get the odd abscess. I know – gums are the last straw in ingratitude. But then it stops.

DON'T GET CAUGHT OUT

One last health remark: at the time of writing, there has been a big increase in middle-aged women of forty and above, some of whom already have grown-up children, having abortions (more than four in ten women, in this age bracket). This is because they think themselves menopausal, or

---

[7] From Vape Emporium, my bricks-and-mortar vaping store of choice (super-friendly and patient; great stock), also online at vapeemporium.com.

perimenopausal, and highly unlikely to get up the duff due to their fertility being in decline. Their periods are erratic at best.

NB: The passage of time is not a safe method of contraception. You can still get pregnant when your fertility is in decline – and, as the figures show, lots of women do. Bpas, formerly the British Pregnancy Advisory Service, now carry out more abortions for women over forty than they do for women under eighteen. **Do not give up using contraception until you're absolutely, 100 per cent sure that your reproductive system has shut down completely.** That's two years after your last period. If in doubt, see your GP.

That's all for now, but see the chapter on the menopause on page 289.

PARTYING

You will know, if you're over the age of about thirty-five(ish), that certain things are no longer possible, chief among them the bender. I mean, it's *possible*, technically, but it takes a minimum of forty-eight hours to recover – sometimes longer – and if you have company, you look so horrendous after a bender that you have to walk around with a brown paper bag on your head, with holes cut out for the eyes, which are full of regret. The aftermath of excess no longer consists of 'I have a headache' on and off over forty-eight hours, it's 'I am worried that I'm going to have a stroke' constantly, for two days straight. In this context, when I say 'a bender' I do not mean a druggy weekend at a music festival but, say, a vaguely boozy lunch that's segued into early-evening drinks (i.e. the sort of thing you used to do perfectly easily when you were young, followed by a quick disco nap, followed by a drunken dinner. And you could still go to work in the morning feeling relatively perky).

Those days are gone. They are *yore*.

Consequently, you can no longer get drunk/take recreational drugs (illegal, so don't do it – except let's not pretend to faint away at the very *idea* that people might, either) just because they're around and you're a bit bored. Standing around wondering whether it would be rude to leave, deciding that yes, it would be, busying yourself by having three big-ass glasses of wine instead: that's out. This, at least, is an excellent thing. Because what it means, in effect, is that, for health reasons, you must only attend social events that are likely to be so enjoyable that you're willing to risk being broken for two days afterwards. This sorts the wheat from the chaff, social life-wise. It narrows things right down.

Alcohol

While your newly streamlined approach to socializing is great, it brings with it a new problem: you become so unused to going out all the time that you also become unused to alcohol, which means the smallest amount makes you sick. So:

* **First rule: only accept invitations to things you really, really want to go to,** non-negotiable close friends and family dos aside.

* **Second rule: try to regulate your drinking,** so that you know your limits and don't take yourself by surprise. I'm all for getting pissed on purpose, but I'm strongly against getting pissed by mistake and suffering the consequences. A good way of regulating your intake is to drink moderately at home, to keep your hand in.

* **Third rule: don't be the woman who can't handle her drink,** the woman who slurs about, banging into things and drunk-flirting.

It is not OK to break this third rule once you're middle-aged, because it doesn't look like you've merely had a few too many: it looks like you've had a few too many *because you're tragic*. I, a champion drinker – and I can still drink most people under the table if I choose to, which I very, very rarely do – have, in recent years, found myself thinking a really terrible thing when I see a very drunk[8] woman who is middle-aged or older. It is:

[8] Or wasted.

'God, she must be so unhappy. Why doesn't she go *home*?' And that's from me – someone who is wholly sympathetic to fully taking advantage of the full-blown night out. Just imagine what other, perhaps more cautious, people are thinking.

I'm sorry for thinking it. I've never thought it before: for decades, I'd think, 'Hahaha, so-and-so's having a good night, worra larf.' But then, one day, at a friend's birthday party, the 'she must be unhappy' thought came into my head about someone, and now I have it quite often. The reason why it is so devastatingly awful is, of course, *pity*. Nobody wants to be pitied – and nobody much wants to do the pitying, either. And yes, it's terribly rock 'n' roll to think, 'Well, if that's what they're thinking, fuck 'em, the squares,' but you see even that sentiment makes me feel pity. Double pity! The horror. Also, the people feeling the pity aren't squares, necessarily. They're just a) wondering why they crossed London to watch you stagger about looking like you might vomit, b) genuinely worried about you, as though you were very old and help-less, and c) sorry for you that you deludedly think you can drink, even though you demonstrably can't. WEAK-LOOK KLAXON.

I think I'm right in my pity. If it's any comfort, I don't go a bundle on pissed middle-aged men, either – but there really is something peculiarly awful about an out-of-control woman in her forties or fifties. (A lone woman, I mean. If every single older person at the party is also drunk-flirting and crashing into things, that's fine, though I am making myself laugh imagining this. Wahey.)

The awfulness is partly to do with 'put it away, Nana' – which, of course, contains within it a mutton component and sets all the bells ringing. But it's also to do with a woman giving the impression that she doesn't get out much, and that her life is so dull and monochrome that on the rare occasions when she does go out, she really 'makes a night of it'. There are all sorts of unspoken implications in this, none of them terrific: boring existence, barren social life, greater or lesser degree of sexual frustration. So bear that in mind.

Am I saying don't get drunk? God, imagine – no, I most certainly am not. (And certainly do what you like in the privacy of your own home.) I'm saying, don't be the woman who everyone feels embarrassed for. Drink, but know enough about yourself to recognize when 'This is such fun' turns into 'I feel like doing sexy dancing by myself now' and then 'Oops, I seem to have fallen over'. In later years, that last one can segue into 'Oh. I can't get up'.

Drugs

My advice here is:

* **Take them in the recovery position, to minimize risk.** Even then, though, mind you don't choke. Invite a friend round to be a sort of minder, maybe.

* **Not in public** – you may be having a good time, but the people watching you will only feel really, really sorry for you. They will not cock their heads and chortle that you're 'a bit of a one'. They will wonder what is wrong with your life. Harsh, I know, but very true. As above, always best to avoid a situation where you are pitied.

* **If you're going to take drugs, take drugs you already know (impeccably sourced).** There are all sorts of new drugs popping up all the time; some are even legal. Nobody wants to see you freaking out as a result of your middle-aged experimentation.

And finally: weed's a lot stronger now than when you were a lad, so bear that in mind.

CHAPTER 6

AILING PARENTS

*How to keep your sanity, and
how to deal with grief*

In the olden days, people routinely used to have children much younger. Today, we sneer at this as being the preserve of the poor and the un-educated, and smugly tell ourselves that we've got it much better sorted, that age brings wisdom and that having children later makes us better parents. That's as may be, but it also means that, depending how late we leave it, we sometimes have no gap at all between the time when parenting our own children ends and parenting our parents begins.

If you were Elsie from the olden days and had your children at the ages of, say, twenty and twenty-two, those children would have reached adulthood by the time you were forty. Say your own mum had you when she was twenty-three: she'd be only sixty-three at this point – in her Prime herself, scooting about doing interesting things. You could relax, and you could relax at length, for years and years.

If you're Charlotte from 2015, it's perfectly possible that you had children when you were aged thirty-eight and forty. These children are teenagers when you're fifty-five. If your mum had you when she was thirty, she's eighty-five now. You see the problem. Elsie, above, had twenty years or so to gad about in, carefree for the first time in her adult life: her children were adults, her parents were still young and able, and she was still a young woman herself. It's different for our generation, who are much more likely to be Charlottes: out of the children frying pan and straight into the aged-parents fire without drawing a breath.

We have robbed ourselves of those carefree years, which were a reward for the parenting years. It's a shame, because God knows we could do with them.

DEALING WITH PARENTAL DECLINE

We can't go back in time and have our children earlier (though I do wish it were possible to have a discussion about the benefits of having children young without everyone freaking out. It's not letting the side down to do something biologically appropriate, for heaven's sake). So we have to deal with what we're given, and very often what we're given is a parent – or two – who's ailing and who relies increasingly heavily upon us. Because surely that's the deal: **your parents cared for you when you were a little child, and you care for them when they become frail**. Fragile, vulnerable, in need of help.

I don't feel that, as a society, we've quite got our

heads around this. There's a general consensus on the idea that if you have a baby, then it's up to you to rear it until it reaches adulthood and can fend for itself. But we do not seem to willingly accept that, as older people decline, it's up to their children to provide a strong arm for them to lean on. You can spend a lot of time in denial about parental decline, thinking surely it's somebody's job to care that your mother appears to have completely lost the plot, casting wildly around for that person – only to realize pretty late in the day that the person is you.

Parental decline is also hard in that, unlike with raising children, you're not there every step of the way. With children, you learn on the job, you master what is required at a particular stage, apply it, carry on, then repeat. With ailing parents, they live their independent lives, as they always have, and any slight deterioration in memory, mobility or personalcarepassesprettymuchunnoticed. Chances are that they don't mention it themselves – because, of course, they're freaked out by it too and may be the kind of people who prefer to pretend it isn't happening – and you, caught up in your own busy life, don't notice. And then one day something un-hideable and unavoidable happens – and bam! Suddenly there it is.

Getting Help

There are precious few guide books for this. Just think of the hundreds – thousands, I expect – of books that have been published about raising babies, children and young people (in that order, which is nuts in itself. Most of the books are about babies – the easiest bit. Some are about children – harder than babies. A few are about young people – the hardest of all). It seems absolutely incredible to me that there aren't hundreds of books about looking after old people. But there aren't. Sure, you may be able to pick up a copy of a book about a specific ailment – *Coping with Dementia*, say, or *After the Fall* (except not by Arthur Miller).[1] But there are no general manuals, no guides, no radio or TV shows, no sitcoms to make you at least feel like you're not alone. There is nothing. Where is the Penelope Leach of geriatrics? Where is the Supernanny of the old? It's particularly extraordinary because every single person on the planet will be called upon to look after their ageing parents at some point. And yet: nothing. A vast sea of silence.

But there is help, all the same.

---

[1] Some facts about falling, from the USA: each year, about 350,000 Americans fall and break a hip. Of those, 40 per cent end up in a nursing home, and 20 per cent are never able to walk again. The three primary risk factors for falling are 1) poor balance, 2) taking more than four prescription medications, and 3) muscle weakness. Elderly people without these risk factors have a 12 per cent chance of falling in a year. Those with all three risk factors have almost a 100 per cent chance (source: *New Yorker*, 2011).

WHERE TO GET HELP

All of the well-known, illness-specific chari-
ties have mostly excellent, informative
websites. But see also, more generally:

- *nhs.uk/carersdirect and gov.uk*
  If your parent is moving in with you,
  have a look at the NHS's online guide.
  This is an excellent portal and a mine
  of information, including information
  about, for example, the forms you need
  to download if your parent needs
  specialist equipment, and about financial entitlements available to you. See
  also the UK government's massive, all-
  encompassing site for services and
  information.

- *carersuk.org*
  The Carers UK website has a very useful
  guide to caring for your elderly parent
  in your home, covering everything from
  money matters to useful gadgets.

- *ageuk.org.uk* and *carerstrust4all.org.uk*
  Age UK and Crossroads Care can help
  older people with shopping, cleaning
  and cooking.

- *independentage.org*
  Independent Age is a 150-year-old
  campaigning charity that offers advice
  and a befriending service to the elderly

across the UK and Ireland, either in person or by phone. They have 1,500 volunteers.

- *nbfa.org.uk*
  NBFA Assisting the Elderly is a charity (established 1957) that helps combat loneliness. They also help carers with respite breaks and offer a telephone monitoring 'check-in' system, so lonely older people don't fall off the radar.

- *aliveactivities.org*
  The jauntily named Alive! was founded in 2009 and goes into 300 care homes to get residents doing stimulating things.

- *fote.org.uk*
  Friends of the Elderly run care homes, day clubs and a befriending service, among other things; the Carers section of the website is full of useful information.

- *thesilverline.org.uk*
  The Silver Line is Esther Rantzen's laudable 24/7 helpline for the elderly (the number is 0800 4 70 80 90), providing information, help or just a friendly chat.

- *cqc.org.uk*
  The Care Quality Commission is the regulator of health and social care in England. The website has inspection reports of various care homes (rather like Ofsted for the older generation).

Breaking the Silence

I know why there's silence about all of this. It's because there's nothing we want to hear. We have our hands over our ears: this stuff is deeper than tears and doesn't bear thinking about. It's because one day, when you have finished looking after your aged parents, you will become like them, and you'll need, and hope, that your children will look after you. In the worst-case scenario, you too will become a vulnerable, dependent baby, asking your children to care for you like you cared for them when they were little. Thinking about this – and I do, a lot – makes me want to run away screaming with my fingers in my ears.

On top of that, babies are cute. You want to look after sweet little babies, all big clear eyes and peachy skin, and you want to change their nappies, and to stay up all night singing them songs when they're teething. Yes, you're knackered, and yes, it's nobody's idea of fun – but what rewards! Your gorgeous little baby, waving chubby little arms and legs, beaming at you. You love him so much your heart could burst.

And as they grow, your babies become less and less vulnerable and helpless. You love and protect them, and they get bigger, stronger, more mentally and physically competent, until one day they turn into glorious adults, and off they skip, out of the door, to live independent lives of their own. Good on you for your excellent parenting! Medals all round!

Old people aren't cute. *Their* gummy smiles and downy-in-the-wrong-way heads don't cause blind adoration, just pity and heart-rending sadness. You can spend months answering a two-year-old whose favourite question is 'Why?' without once losing your temper. An old person – *your* old person, who loves you so much, who grew you and raised you – asking the same thing more than twice just makes you feel irritated. You reassure children cheerfully and tirelessly; you reassure old people, for the umpteenth time, with tension or weariness in your voice. And your elderly parents are only going to get more vulnerable and more helpless, less physically and mentally able. You're going to care for them as they deteriorate and then die. Yes, you are. No wonder this conversation fills so many of us with utter panic.

How I hate the contempt we feel towards age – although I am not immune to feeling it, too. I hate the way we – I – use 'old' as an insult, as shorthand for: 'Throw yourself in the bin, why don't you?' If someone is very rude to me on Twitter, do you know what I do? I go and look at their picture, gauge their age, then sometimes reply with reference to their decrepitude and senility, ergo obvious lack of comprehension. I make the suggestion that they are too doddery and ancient to see the joke or point. It's really revolting of me, and it's a total knee-jerk reaction.

'Stupid old git,' I mutter to myself. 'Mad old bat.' 'Piss off, grandad.'

Where does it even come from, this age-directed venom? Nobody speaks like that around me, in my normal home life. And I don't think I've ever been exposed to 'elder contempt' while around my friends or family. It just seeps in. In the same way that we pity young women for constantly being subjected to a drip-drip of sexism (some of it unwitting), I really pity us for whom 'old' snuck in as a term of abuse while we weren't even looking.

Coming to Terms with Our Anger

How awful all of this is, and how terrible is the un-brave panic that fills us at the idea of a parent becoming hopelessly vulnerable. How bad it makes us feel – we, who think of ourselves as loving daughters and kind, compassionate human beings. Short-temperedness and irritation – what is *wrong* with us? We know how to be patient – or how to feign patience, brilliantly – from having had small children. But now it's needed, we can't summon it up – not really, not convincingly – or only in short bursts. We stick a smile on, and a cheerful voice, and we cut the dinner up into teeny little pieces, like a grotesque parody of readying a baby for solids, but inside we are feeling resentful and aggrieved.

Sometimes we are angry too (and see page 126 for an explanation of how anger and fear often

207

come from the same place). When my late father got Alzheimer's, I don't think there are words to describe how angry – livid, furious, incandescent – I felt. I felt anger towards the disease, obviously. I felt anger at the world, at a God I don't necessarily believe in, at stupid bloody medicine that can give people new genders but couldn't give my father back his marbles, of which there used to be many – half his marbles would have done. A quarter. Six. Anything rather than seeing him gaga, tied to a chair – because he was not benign in his dementia, he was not 'content' or 'placid' or 'away with the fairies'; he saw only demons. He was enraged and constantly wanting to run – through rooms, through doors, through windows made of glass. I can't say I blamed him.

But what a sight: restrained, in a room full of terrifyingly bonkers old people, shouting, wearing an adult nappy. My dad the shagger, the drinker, so brilliantly funny, so clever, who loved motorbikes and maps and road trips and eating and history and chess. My dad, who spoke four languages, now speechlessly grinding his teeth with rage, rocking. My dad in that chair, and me, in my early thirties, his only child, thinking, like a selfish monster, 'This is unfair. This is not what I deserve.' He was so mighty, and so fallen, and it made me so angry that I didn't even feel that sad. Just cross. Yes, with him, too. It had been a long time since I'd thought him infallible, but I never thought him weak. And now this: not only fallible, but broken. What a thing to do to me, I thought.

As the only child of a man I hadn't shared a roof with since I was two and basically only knew – and loved, though – from the school holidays, the burden of care seemed disproportionate. Also, the burden of paying for his nursing home had an enormous impact on my young family's finances (my dad's sister helped, thank God – I don't know what I'd have done otherwise). That situation must happen more and more these days, now that families are so often complicated: the parent who got custody dies, you carry on with life, you're maybe close to your live-in step-parent . . . and then the biological parent gets very ill. I knew my dad, because my mother had ensured that we saw each other as often as school, aeroplanes and geography allowed. But what if she'd been one of those mothers that discouraged contact?

When the biological parent has become estranged, you would still rush to the bedside, probably – but then what? You would barely know this person who gave you life. Of course you would try to bring them comfort. Tricky, though, if you'd never actually set foot in their house, didn't know what books they liked or what their favourite colour was.

And what of the parent who was terrible to you – the absolute bastard of a parent that was violent, abusive, sadistic or worse until you managed to get away? Are you supposed to effect a deathbed reconciliation, and bless them as they leave this earth? You're not, you know. Where parents are monsters, it's fine to cut them loose, and it's fine to feel absolutely zero guilt about doing so. Do what your conscience dictates, and then move on.

Liking our parents to be strong, and hating to see them looking frail, is the worst bit about ageing, I think: few things are sadder than a force of nature being cut down to size or a blaze sputtering into a damp squib. A friend of mine says: 'I was very angry with my father in his last eighteen months: I just hated him for being feeble, instead of this huge, polarizing, larger-than-life figure. When we went on holiday with him six weeks before he died, he seemed to find everything an effort. My shameful reaction was to be irritated. When you are old and ill, everything *is* a gigantic effort, but it can make a grown-up child feel irrationally, and unforgivably, cross. We don't like the physical frailty and, worse still, **the disgustingness of the very old**. We all know it is unreasonable, but we can't help ourselves. I think we are scared because underneath we know that we're next.'

Staying Positive

This chapter, as you can see, is jolliness itself. I should insert joke breaks, really.[2] Bear in mind,

[2] If you want to read something deeply moving and depressing but also wonderful and hilarious about the

though, that I am deliberately presenting horrible scenarios. Some very old people remain absolutely themselves, full of verve and vigour, and die peacefully in their sleep at a grand old age.

Only about 15 per cent of old people lose their marbles – incredibly cheering, really (from the media coverage, you could be forgiven for thinking that it's about one in two). The most common causes of death are stroke, heart disease and cancer. Most of the things we as middle-aged children have, or may have, to deal with are ailments such as deafness, cataracts, macular degeneration (problems with central vision where the thing you're directly looking at appears blurred), arthritis, Parkinson's, treatable coronary disease and lungs packing up – plus the aftermath of those terrible falls.

It's awful, and it's sad, but all of these conditions can be helped and remedied to varying degrees: they are amenable to treatment. Start with the NHS website, then the ailment-specific charity, and take a look through the list of other resources earlier in this chapter on page 203.

The recurring difficulty for those looking after ailing parents is what to do if it appears the family doctor does not know precisely what is amiss – or could, indeed, have overlooked some potentially

―――――
whole topic of ailing parents, I strongly recommend graphic artist Roz Chast's brilliantly drawn (in both senses) memoir *Can't We Talk About Something More Pleasant?*

treatable problem. There are two important issues here:

* The elderly are prone to having **several different medical problems simultaneously**. This can lead to them being referred to a medley of different medical specialists, but it is often preferable in this situation to suggest they see a geriatrician who is better able to take a broad all-round view of what is going on and to advise appropriately.

* It is not unusual for them to be taking **half a dozen or more different medications**: to lower the blood pressure, cholesterol and blood sugar levels, strengthen the bones, etc. This carries the substantial risk of side effects that can exacerbate the symptoms of ageing, causing muscular aches and pains, difficulty in concentrating and general malaise. The cardinal rule here is 'less is more' – the fewer medications taken the better – and it is not unusual for someone to feel a whole lot better after reducing the number of medicines they are taking.

Finally, it can be helpful when ailing parents are having difficulty coping at home to seek the advice of an occupational therapist to suggest a range of kitchen or bathroom devices, as well as specially designed beds and chairs that will improve matters.

DEALING WITH DEMENTIA

There are lots of nicer scenarios than the lingering horrors I have been describing, and they are scenarios where the dominant emotion is sorrow alone. But I am now going to focus on dementia, the reason being that it is the most painful example of dealing with an ailing parent – because on top of everything else, your parent, the parent you loved, has *gone*. That is not the case with, say, cancer and other serious illnesses, distressing as they are. I also think that dementia is a good gateway through which to approach more closely the difficult subject of anger and irritation that we sometimes feel towards old people we love. So many people feel it, and the guilt of it can be absolutely tormenting. It might be a comfort to know that those suffering from such guilt are not alone, and that their feelings – their unlovely feelings – are not abnormal. (Mind you, saintly people do exist, and they're at a major advantage here. Oh, how I admire them, and how I wish I was one of them. And how inexpressibly grateful I am to them when they pop up in a medical context. Geriatric nurses! Actual angels, walking among us.)

Some thoughts, though, first:

* **Women seem to have more complicated feelings about ailing parents than men.** It seems that men can't bear the pathos of parents in decline. They can't bear the distress their

loved ones are in. But they're arguably more straightforward than women when it comes to the difficult emotions: I don't know that they experience them to the same extent. They feel sad and sorry, and that's broadly it. It's more than enough, and it rather suggests they are either kinder or more patient. Women, I think, feel a whole slew of other stuff, too – perhaps because they are more closely involved with managing their parents' decline.

* **I know people who long for a parent to be dead,** because the parent's decline is so slow and agonizing – for the parent, for the parent's spouse and for their adult children. It's OK to feel like this: lots of people do. Sometimes the parent is relentlessly negative and critical, and basically hates everything and everybody, all of the time – including you and including your children. It's worth calling the parent out on this, as you might call out a bully at school. (We might pause here to note how horrendous relentless negativity is, and how it can eventually eat away all of the good and nice things about a person, so that only this puddle of bile is left. Sometimes you can see it coming. It's for this reason that I personally avoid people my age whose pessimism and anger become the dominant characteristics as they age, and harder and harder to ignore. This sounds a bit hippieish – bad vibes, bad karma – but I don't care: it's true.)

★ **Force yourself, if that's what it takes, to spend as much time as possible with elderly parents.** You will be bereft when they are gone – even if your relationship was imperfect, even if you weren't especially close, even if everything. **Losing a parent, even as an ageing grown-up, is never less than devastating, even when it is also a relief.** If you do have a difficult relationship with a parent (which means you'll probably be stuck at the anger stage for longer than someone whose relationship was un-fraught and easy), fix it, whatever it takes. Swallow all your pride; tell white lies; be *good*. Force yourself. Kindness is better for everybody – you included – than rage (easier said than done, I know). There can be few worse things than someone dying and you not having patched things up with them. That stuff haunts you worse than any ghost.

ON DEMENTIA

Dementia is especially, sometimes unbearably, difficult, because the person you loved – your mother or father – has gone, and been replaced with another person, who may be unloveable. Sometimes the person you used to know may pop up and say hello before being dragged beneath the waves again, but sometimes not: they're gone for good. It is unbelievably upsetting. It's even more upsetting if your compassion is tempered with dislike, and even hatred, of this new person.

'I loved my mother,' says a friend. 'She was brilliant, funny, glamorous and sharp, and also difficult, spiky and argumentative. It wasn't the easiest relationship even then. But she was *fun*. That person disappeared, and I hated the one who appeared instead. After the dementia, Mum was just difficult and spiky – not sharp at all and certainly not glamorous or fun. Conversation with her was so arduous: she never went anywhere, so she had nothing to say.[3]

'Later, it was a bit like having a conversation with someone who is on the brink of going to sleep or sinking underwater all the time – disjointed and woozy. She would lose the thread constantly. If you told her what you had been doing, she needed everything explained, or she just contradicted you – "I'm eighty-three" said when she was ninety, or "No, I don't know Jane"

---

[3] This can be true of old people regardless of dementia. Agitate like mad to make sure that your parents have hobbies and interests, even if it's only an addiction to soap operas – anything, as long as you can talk about it. Remember that a small world makes for a small mind, and a small mind makes for a tiny world. Encourage old people to think big, bold thoughts and not to let their horizons shrink away to nothing.

(her best friend), or "No, I have never been there" of somewhere she'd been hundreds of times. You're told never to contradict the demented, but it is hard not to, when you're told that your 21-year-old is in fact eight. When I did contradict her – "No, Mum, he's twenty-one" – she'd sulkily say, "Well, if you say so."' (This was probably not remotely amusing for my friend at the time, but I chortled typing it. Humour is your greatest ally in these situations. It may be pitch-black, but it's your life raft and your personal emergency service. Ya really do actually gotta larf.)

Another friend says, of her dad: 'In the last couple of years he sometimes didn't recognize me, or painfully mistook me for one of his friends – a friend he really didn't like. He was always astonished when told my age (he thought I was about thirty-six). And, worst of all, he lost that inhibitor thing we all have. He would say some devastating things: "I have always loved your sister more than you," or, "It's such a shame you're so fat."' Disinhibition can result in very wounding things being said – things that wound all the more for sometimes having the ring of truth about them. My dad once glared at me and said, not in a friendly way, 'Who are you?' It was a good question. The correct answer ('Your only child, the one who left when she was nine and changed her name when she was fourteen, the one who lives and works in another language, the one who doesn't actually know you – any version of you – all that brilliantly') seemed more long-winded and existential than was called for.

You have to force yourself to see these uninvited revelations, such as they are, as both funny and mad. The worst thing you can possibly do is sit and brood over them and try to analyse them. They come from a place of madness. There is no point in trying to apply logic. Nasty punch, but you have to roll with it. Also, don't make your woundedness known – by the time you express it, your parent may not remember saying the initial thing, and will just feel (extra) baffled and confused. Never use sarcasm – in my friend's example above, 'That's good, because my sister loves you more than I do' – for the same reason: you can't be sarcastic with someone who may not understand what you're being sarcastic about. You can be sarcastic in your head, though. The internal monologue really comes into its own here. It may also help to write it all down, on the Unsent Letter/ Deleted Email principle: it's not actually doing anything, but it makes you feel a lot better to have got it off your chest.

Weird changes in character can also happen. Someone I knew, with the most savoury tooth in the world – she couldn't abide sugar or sweet things – started eating only biscuits and chocolate and drinking Liebfraumilch. I'd say, 'Can I bring you anything?' and she'd say, 'Yes, cake.' And I'd say, 'Really? But you hate and despise cake.' 'I do not,' she would exclaim, looking triumphant. Oddly, along with this newfound passion for sweetness, she – a brisk sort, to put it mildly – became treaclishly sentimental.

Another friend remarks that her mother, who'd spent her life being a stylish dresser and who was the sort of woman who owned a bright pink satin skirt and many an It bag, suddenly developed an unquenchable thirst for beige clothing.

'For the last five years of her life, going to see my mum was like the worst torture,' says the friend I was quoting earlier. 'And of course I did see her – she was my mum. I saw her once a week at least. I hated it and I hated the person I went to see, who so obviously wasn't her. Thank God for my sister, as there were massive jokes – we used to call her Lady Gaga – and we could commiserate about it. We'd talk about how we couldn't believe she wasn't dead yet. And how we longed for her to be dead. It seems so awful when I put it like that, out loud – but that's how it was. Gallows humour.'

See, jokes again. So important. Siblings are invaluable allies here. Speaking of siblings, it is also inevitable that the work of caring for a parent will probably not be divided perfectly equally between you. It is an absolute waste of time to harbour resentments about this, whether you're the one who's doing more or the one who's doing less. Having said that, never tell a sibling that they're doing more than you are because they're 'better' at it. It's possible, but they may equally be just as distressed as you and merely better at forcing themselves to get on with it with minimal fuss. Being told that you're 'better' at coping with unpleasant stuff is insanely irritating in any circumstance, but espe-cially so here. Nobody is 'better' at cleaning up poo, for instance, than anyone else. You're not born with a poo-cleaning gene.

Here are some dementia specifics, though obviously symptoms will vary from person to person:

* **'The onset of dementia was the worst bit** – for about three or four years she was acutely anxious and angry about everything. Some-times she would say during this period "I'm

completely poggled[4] now" but we knew she was just testing us to say no, of course you're not. And after a bit we couldn't. She wasn't stupid – she knew. Which made it even worse.'

* **'We took over doing the things that made her especially anxious** – paying the bills, buying presents for grandchildren's birthdays, eventually buying presents for our own birthdays.'

* **'There was a terrible time with my dad where, when you had visited him, he begged you to take him home with you.** He was just frightened of being on his own.' This is like my dad's impulse to run, Forrest Gump-like, out of his nursing home and all the way to . . . Where? It is absolutely awful but it seems standard – everyone I know in this situation has been begged by their parent to either spring them out of hospital/a care home or to come and live with them. The much-lauded Mediterranean/Eastern model – all the generations together under one roof – is all well and good provided you have the room, and provided you have no concerns about safety (such as someone with dementia making themselves a snack and accidentally setting the house on fire). It's a lovely idea

---

[4] Hardly the time or place, but 'poggled' is an excellent word.

– the communal living, not the fire – and it would be lovely if everyone could manage it, but they can't. That doesn't mean that old people's loneliness isn't decimating and terrible: seek solutions (and see page 203).

* **More on disinhibition** (from a fourth friend, this time): 'There were terrible social pitfalls. She would take herself to a gallery opening, or a party, or a funeral, or even just an evening with a friend and something would happen. I never knew quite what – she never wanted to talk about it – but it would result in her having to be taken home. I suspect she didn't recognize people she knew very well, or argued with people, or got lost, or looked lost. At this point, when it would have been good to have been able to sit and discuss what was happening to her – I couldn't. My brother tried, too. But, no go. She would deflect and defer that conversation so rigorously that we never had it. She was still very clever underneath the dementia, and she would do everything she could to try to avoid you seeing it. She never, *ever* wanted to talk about it. Her doctor told us that she did know: she had discussed it with him.'

This is the thing I most fear for myself – the dawning realization that you're losing your marbles, the intolerable pathos of trying to pretend that it isn't happening, the clinging to normal life – yes, of course I can go to that party or that gallery opening, don't be silly, why wouldn't I? – and then having to be rescued from it by an exasperated adult child ('Mum! We were in the middle of dinner!'), with you too ashamed to even attempt to explain what went wrong, if indeed you *can* even explain.

As for never having the conversation: this breaks my heart for everybody concerned. I wouldn't want to have the conversation either, if I were going loopy. What do you possibly say, without starting to cry with fear? 'I'm afraid I'm going mad. More tea?'

* **If your parent is compos mentis enough to have a mobile phone and keep it charged** (or if you have the foresight to give it a charge, turn it on and stick it in their handbag/coat pocket when you visit), then it's a very good idea to install a tracker app on to it, so that you always know exactly where he or she is. Bear in mind that the next generation of eighty-somethings will have had a mobile for much of their adult lives, so your parent's iPhone could be a useful everyday aid in dealing with dementia.

* **Use carers, if you can possibly afford it:** spend your inheritance, should you be lucky enough to have one; take out a mortgage on your parents' property (or on your own, pending the sale of theirs). 'One thing I feel great pride

about is that in the nine years that followed her diagnosis of dementia, my mum was able to stay in her own flat,' a friend says. 'It used up all her remaining money, but it was worth it. The carers were and are amazing people: we almost never had a bad one in all that time. They were the least despising, kindest people imaginable, and how they could stand to be alone with her in the hot stuffy flat I can't imagine. But they could, and all she wanted was to stay at home. I feel happy knowing that she got her wish.'[5] Few things are sadder than someone begging to go home and being told that they can't, or being lied to about how it might happen 'next week' or 'when you're a bit better'. If there are funds that can be used to pay for a carer, then use them.

* **Two practical points:** 1) Get power of attorney good and early – as soon as it becomes clear that the person can't manage bills, money or decisions; 2) Take independent financial advice if you are going to have to fund long-term care.

* **Two things to look out for:** 1) malnutrition and 2) depression. Both need to be treated. The former is very common and sometimes accidental. Older people do have smaller

[5] My friend recommends Consultus Care (consultuscare.com).

appetites, but nobody can function properly on half a tin of tomato soup for lunch and a weedy slice of bread and butter for supper. If you're in charge of the shopping, make sure the food you buy is nutritious as well as nice to eat. Sneak calories in, if need be – double cream in the scrambled eggs, and so on.

The Value of Experience

Now, more cheerfully, think how often you say to yourself: 'Yes, I'm older than I was, but man – I know a shitload of stuff.' Don't be afraid to make the same observation about your parents. It's very easy to think, 'Oh, she's going off on her usual rant about her usual topic,' and to slightly zone out.

If a person's life is quiet and un-busy, and if they don't have many interests, the tried-and-tested rant on the tried-and-tested subject must always be tempting. But you're not powerless – you can steer them away from it and into properly fascinating territory.

Your aged parents are twenty or thirty years older than you – they are, whether they know it or not, a repository of amazing stories. They have the long view. My human understanding of the Second World War, for example, was shaped entirely by my grandmother and the stories she loved telling. My interest in these waned when I became a teenager, sadly and unforgivably, but how I'd love to hear them again now, when it's too late, and to ask better questions. This also applies to questions regarding our own family: there are so many fascinating stories. Why did one of my great-aunts become a nun for a while? What about another great-aunt, whose only daughter was killed, along with her children, by her (the daughter's) insane husband?[6] And what happened to the insane husband?

My dad had such an interesting life, and I asked him about so little of it. And now, of course, it's much too late, and it makes me sad.

You are so, so sorry when they are gone.

CELEBRATING LIFE

And so to death: or rather, to **the supreme importance of an excellent funeral**. I can't state this strongly enough. A good funeral is your chance to wipe away all of the grim latter bits and to remember and celebrate your beloved parent as they really were, in their golden Prime, when things were simpler and you were all happy (if only you'd realized it at the time, eh? Carpe diem).

[6] This great-aunt, you will be pleased to hear, remarried (she'd been widowed) at eighty and was blissfully, deliriously happy until the end of her life. She and her husband were always snogging – not in a gross way, but he'd goose her bottom – and they were always going for naked swims in the bleak North Sea. I found it incredibly unseemly when I was thirteen but am now grinning delightedly at the memory. They were massively into each other. It's never too late.

I can't bear bad funerals – and there are so many of those: half-arsed, perfunctory, poorly organized. They appal me in their disrespectfulness. You are saying goodbye to *a whole human life*. It's the last thing you'll ever do for the parent to whom you owe your entire existence. See them out with a bang. You should, for instance, really be able to do better than a vicar who never met the person and whose platitudinous eulogy makes that crystal clear. (Having said that, platitudes have their place, in church. They can be very comforting and reassuring in their unoriginality, like a mug of hot milk.) And you can always do better than gross sandwiches that curl up.

Or maybe you can't, because you're too sad – in which case, delegate, but delegate to somebody competent. All those people saying 'If there's anything I can do' usually mean it: take them up on their kind offers. Get the one who's a good cook to organize the food and refreshments, get the keen gardener to sort out the flowers, and so on. Or do it yourself: it's good therapy and at these times it really *is* good to keep busy.

NB: I don't quite know how one would broach this – perhaps it would have to be volunteered – but do try to get a sense of what the ailing parent would like at their funeral. Some people are happy – keen, even – to discuss this; others leave detailed instructions in their will. The best funerals tend to have the deceased's imprimatur, so that it can feel like they're in the room – which, of course, they are. Readings, hymns, music: it's so much better if it really is 'what they would have wanted'.

Organizing a Good Funeral

If there are no instructions set down, throw a party to follow the service/cremation/ceremony.

*   **The party can be for 200 people or for 6:** it doesn't matter.

*   **It can be wherever you want it to be:** in the pub, your house, your parent's favourite field, whatever.

*   **Make sure that there is plenty to drink:** very good, strong tea (weak tea, weak mind, I always think) and plenty of it; soft drinks for any children attending and any adults who want that; and alcohol for those who'd prefer that and feel fortified by it.

*   **Make an effort with the food,** because the better the food (and drink), the longer people will stay.

All this matters, because what you really want to avoid is people paying their respects and then legging it as soon as possible. A good wake is one where people loosen up, start reminiscing and telling funny stories, and where you feel the *spirit* of the person – the essence of their self – is really being celebrated.

Here is my friend from earlier again, on the subject of her mother's funeral: 'What was remarkable was how 150 people turned up: all these people who had deserted her – or whom she had pushed away – in the dementia years. We had pictures of her in her Prime everywhere, and it was wonderful because looking at all the photographs suddenly recaptured how wonderful and glamorous she was, and what an extraordinary life she had lived. The sad grey pudding lying in a bed disappeared out of my head, and I only remembered her as lovely.'

Making Sure No One is Left Out

Another friend recently attended the funeral of her former stepfather, who for various complicated reasons – mostly to do with mental illness – had fallen through the cracks, ending up very much on his uppers, and with whom she was no longer in touch. A neighbour of this man's – an everyday saint, really – went through every single number in the stepfather's address book and rang up every one. As a result of this act of pure kindness, the funeral was packed with people from every stage of his life, including people who'd been at *primary school* with him. It was, by all accounts, the most fantastic service, and there was the most fantastic party afterwards in the pub.

People left feeling sad that he had died, of course, but also weak with laughter and fondness at various shared anecdotes about him, and filled with love for him. That's what you want. And to think that, had it not been for the neighbour's dedication to the task, he'd have had one of those desperate funerals with only two attendees.

That's the other thing about funerals: it's very important to publicize them. Not everyone reads the papers, even the local ones, and not everyone hears of a death in time. The best way really is to go through the address or contacts book. If you can't hack it yourself, it's the perfect job for a young person – a grown-up grandchild would be ideal.

I hope I'm not putting undue emphasis on numbers. It doesn't matter if the funeral is minute, as is often the case with very old people whose friends and contemporaries are mostly dead – *blows party tooter* – or with people who just had quiet, unsocial lives. All that matters is that the funeral does justice to the person.

A bad funeral is a horrible thing. A good funeral helps the living to recover, and to feel sad in a truly happy way.[7]

[7] I recently went to my friend's mum's funeral. Her coffin – traditional shape, rigid sides – was made out of wool. It was beautiful, and appropriate because she was a champion knitter, but also it was so comforting – lovely, blankety wool, rather than hard wood. You felt that she was cosy in there, tucked in rather than laid out.

CHAPTER 7

OLD FRIENDS, NEW FRIENDS, GOOD FRIENDS, BAD FRIENDS

And changing relationships

Jerry Seinfeld said a brilliant thing in a 2014 interview. It was that his favourite part of the Emmy Awards was when the comedy writers went on stage to pick up their gong. 'You see these gnome-like cretins, just kind of all misshapen. And I go, "This is me. This is who I am. That's my group."' And he was bang on. At our age, you don't care about impressing new people, or surrounding yourself with cool ones. You just want your group. That doesn't mean your group can't be added to, though. It just means you know what future group members are likely to be like. It saves an awful lot of time.

SAVOURING OLD FRIENDS

I'm still friends with some of the people I was at school with thirty-five years ago. It's not like I hang out with them all the time: we see each other two or three times a year. But there's that weird and amazing thing you have with people who you've known forever: instant connectedness and intimacy, as if you'd last seen them yesterday. You talk in a sort of accelerated shorthand, even after all this time. Mind you, these are friends from when I was at boarding school, and I do think that has something to do with it. When you live with people 24/7, the friendships you make are cut from an especially sturdy cloth (like the gross pants – Blue Bags – we had to wear for gym).

For me, the oldest friendships are also the simplest. People I've known for thirty-five years know exactly what I'm like, since my basic character is more or less the same now as it was at fifteen – give or take my great wisdom (joke) and the baggage I've acquired along the way. Because we don't see each other very often, and because we used to know each other so well, we cut to the chase when we do meet up: there's no dancing around the edges of particular topics. These friendships are very satisfying, and put paid to the notion that you have to see someone three times a week in order to feel close to them.

Old friendships (and even newer ones) are often a casualty of marriage, or relationships, at our age. Unless you both absolutely adore a person *and* that person's partner – and that person's children, ideally[1] – they can fall by the wayside. While that

---

[1] Very much not a given, that last one. One of the great mysteries of life is how people you really like can have quite dislikeable children.

is sometimes inevitable, it's also a shame. I'm against the idea that real friends have to be fully incorporated into your family life, that they have to join you for Sunday lunch and bring everyone, that they have to come and stay for a weekend with their partner. If you like your friend, but don't go a whole hog on her boring husband, **do try to maintain the solo friendship**. It isn't good (or nice) to dump, or slow-dump, one's friends for one's relationship – something that people often discover the hard way when said relationship ends and they look around them and see that they have thrown away all their friends, incautiously. And anyway, it's lovely to have lunch with a girlfriend, sans partners: it's one of the great joys of life, and one of the great joys, especially, of late middle age.

CANCELLING A DATE

To middle-aged me, there is no greater joy than someone – even someone I really, really love – cancelling a date. The date was made ages ago in a spirit of optimism, but now it's drizzling outside, you've had a frantic day, and you would like nothing more than to make a nest on the sofa and just sort of *mill about*. Instead, you have to take a shower, do your face, get dressed again and head out into the Outside World, where you'll have to be charming and attentive and make conversation. What utter woe. Happily, everyone starts loving cancelling at around our age.

When I get texts from a friend saying, 'Are we still on? I don't mind AT ALL if you want to cancel,' I know that friend is longing for the same quiet night in as I am. Sometimes I cancel friends and they go, 'YAY! I'm so happy!' at the news. This only happens with intimate friends, obviously – I don't recommend exploding with joy when someone you know less well blows you out. But all my close friends know I love to cancel, and to be cancelled, and they feel exactly the same way.

Sometimes we're planning a night out and one of us will say, 'I just don't have the energy,' and everybody understands. Not one person goes, 'Oh no, what a disaster.' This is utter heaven.

To me, cancelling is like giving me a present. It is worth more than rubies. Boyfriend, box set, bowl of pasta: my idea of heaven. The truth of the matter is, I can't bear going out any more (see page 253).

The Invisible Friendship Expiry Date

Not all friendships survive the passing years. Some friends are time-specific, and should have a 'best before' date: the friend you went raving with in the late eighties (and who you have nothing at all

234

in common with, other than liking dancing in fields); the friend who lived in your street fifteen years ago; the friend who was a mum at school and whose interests dovetailed perfectly with yours when your children were aged between five and eleven. I'm not suggesting you dump all of these people, but I certainly think that, as life whizzes by, there are inevitable casualties.

These years, now, should be about pleasurable things and pleasurable people. **There are enough sad things going on around the edges,** as we saw in the previous chapter. Friendship should bring joy and never feel like a chore. That's never been truer than in these years of our Prime.

I have realized in the process of writing this chapter that, for me, the friends who have somehow fallen by the wayside tend to be:

* **the ones who don't have children,** broadly speaking (there are exceptions), and

* **the ones who are permanently single and aggressively unhappy about it** (I have many happily single friends who don't bang on about their singleness every minute that God sends).

This makes perfect sense: there is nothing duller for a childless person than someone talking about their children – or about any of the child-related extensions, such as schools, contagious diseases or exams. Equally, if you do have kids and if your life is necessarily filled with stuff – children, grand-children, all of that – then there is no especial pleasure to be had in a single and/or childless person banging on about the minutiae of their small, unpeopled life. Often these people are rather self-dramatizing, and it can come across as the worst kind of narcissism. It's because they have so much time to think about themselves. (I'd have rather died than said this out loud when I was younger – even though I thought it then, too. But I am older now, and I don't care.)

I've also noticed, oddly, that childless people talk about their parents all the time, and about their own childhoods. It's not that interesting. I'm not saying that talking about your own children is that interesting either, mind you. I'm saying that people with similar lives tend to pod together in the end.

Culling Bad Friends

Being out of step with your friends is an unpleasant feeling on both sides. The problem is also that it can happen so quickly. One minute you're, say, party-loving and gregarious, the next you want nothing more than to stay at home, pottering about (pottering! One of the GREAT JOYS of life). Or one minute you're the very incarnation of some-body urban and metropolitan, the next you announce you're moving to the country – you, who can barely tell a cow from a seal (and see page 271). Meanwhile your old mucker, whose interests used

236

to tally perfectly with yours, is wondering whether you're having some sort of prolonged episode. Why don't you want to go out? Why are you trying to make her look at pictures of cows/seals? Why aren't you desperate to knock back the martinis and settle in for a good gossip any more?

We're like cheeses, I think. Some of us mature differently than others. With some cheeses – a Gruyère, say – maturity occurs, but the basic aspect stays the same. With some others – Brie, I'm thinking – the actual structure of the Brie changes with the passage of time. Once firm and knife-repelling, it's now oozing all over the plate. The problems occur if you're a Gruyère and your friend is a Brie, or vice versa. While we're on food metaphors, some people mature like wine, getting progressively more delicious, and some turn to vinegar, I'm afraid, causing you to want to spit them out. These are the people you must cull.

VAMPIRE FRIENDS

You know those people you've known for ages and have been friends with for years, except that you're never happy to see them? You can barely remember why you're friends in the first place. You never especially look forward to your meetings with them, and afterwards you go home feeling oddly deflated and demoralized, possibly even depressed. They seem to suck the joy out of any situation. They've always got loads of things they want to moan about. If you have good news, they never seem particularly pleased for you. If you have bad news, they get competitive, and instead of commiserating with you, they try to trump your bad news with bad news of their own. They feed off your life-force and send you home completely drained.

You've probably felt like that about a particular friend for ages. But there are loads of 'buts'. But she was once very kind to you and you feel you owe her. But it's not her fault that she's so miserable (it is, actually). But she's had a run of bad luck recently. But her cat's lost. But her husband's left her (surprise!). But she's a difficult person and she doesn't have many friends – only you, really. But she has a gammy leg. But she's had a health scare. But, but, but . . .

It's time to toughen up. If a person makes you feel like crap every single time you see them – if there is no joy whatsoever in any encounter you have with them – then the time has come to make an exit. Often it's not only that there's no joy – as if that weren't bad enough – but that the person also causes you actual *distress* in some way, in a manner that may be presented as guileless but that you suspect may be malicious: she somehow always has you-specific bad news to impart. The reason for wanting to cause you distress is that the person resents either the whole of you, or some aspect of your life. These people are awful – they're the pits – and yet for some reason we all have one or two of them in our lives.

Cull them. It's a kindness to everybody.

These friends don't love you, and God knows you don't love them. If all they bring to the party is discomfort and misery – well, off they go, into the bin. It's your life, and you're more than halfway through it.

Choose happiness. Choose people who enhance your day, not human rainclouds.

Shelving Annoying Friends

The need for culling often becomes manifest when you're going through a stressful or difficult period within your own family, and you feel that you can really do without spending your precious spare time in the company of somebody who's basically a dog, with you as the lamp post. Don't cull, though, when all that's required is **small withdrawal**. Social media is brilliant for this: it's great for maintaining friendships, full stop. But also for maintaining the illusion of an intimacy that's greater than the actuality.

Some friends, for instance, go a bit mad at one

time or another – maybe around the menopause, maybe not – and here I am thinking of my friend who had the unfunniest of funny turns and briefly proposed to marry a man who was two years older than her son. Then one morning she woke up and thought, 'How extraordinary, I went completely loony there for three months.' And then it was all fine.

She blames the menopause, but there are lots of things that can make you go a bit wonky, chief among them the realization that the period of you being relatively young is drawing, or has drawn, to a close. And of course when that realization dawns, you look around you and think, 'Blimey, is this it?' If you're pleased with what you find, great. But not everyone is, hence the occasionally drastic changes in lifestyle that can occur.

Anyway, my solution to all of these woes – mad friends, friends who become histrionic, friends whom it's somehow not as easy being friends with as it used to be – is social media. You may think it's not for you, you may think that all it consists of is people inanely discussing their breakfasts (nobody has done this since 2009, but never mind), or that there's no imaginable benefit to be gained from joining a particular site. Do reconsider. Social media can be incredibly useful – and if you're intimidated by the level of techy competence it requires, don't be. Being friends with someone via Facebook or Twitter is easy. With a few clicks of your mouse, you can tell your friend that you like what she's saying, what she's wearing, her cup of morning coffee and her dogs. You can laugh at her jokes and answer her queries. The overlap between the real world and the online world is so thin these days – really, they're pretty much one and the same. It is extremely useful.

If you are reading this and thinking, 'Yes, that makes sense, but unfortunately I'm absolutely useless with computers,' then please don't. There is no heroism in being a Luddite. There is nothing charming about not understanding 'computers'. The rest of us all like real books and real letters too, and it's very tiresome when people announce this preference as if it somehow makes them special. (That's what it is, by the way, this refusal to engage with technology. It's a way of saying: 'I am too special to understand. My mind is simply too original, you see, to bother itself with this stuff.' It makes you look very silly. Also, I don't understand the lack of curiosity. Why wouldn't someone who uses the internet at even the most perfunctory level – sending emails, Skyping – want to learn what to do if it suddenly stops working? It's like having a fountain pen and making panicked phone calls when it runs out of ink. You could just learn to change the cartridge.)

MAKING NEW FRIENDS

So now you've culled the bad friends and gently shelved the annoying ones – take heart, it's not as brutal as it sounds – you might want to cultivate some new ones. Or, of course, you might not: you might think, 'Thank Christ for that, a bit of peace and quiet.' Let's assume the former, though, because new friends are exciting. I didn't think this until quite recently. On the contrary, I thought, 'I have all the friends I need, and I don't even manage to see those as much as I'd like to. I therefore have zero interest in meeting new people. My friend cupboard is full – there's nowhere to put new ones.'

In reality, there's always room for a few more – especially if you make space using the methods described above.

Embracing Social Media

If you're lonely, or if you're in a new place, or if you're just bored and fancy some fresh blood, I recommend getting online. If your interests tally with someone you meet on social media – and if they make you laugh and say interesting things and generally seem *really* likeable – then it's usually worth giving them a punt in real life.

Be aware, though, that this can go very wrong, as well as very right. I don't mean in a 'hit over the head with an axe' way, more in a disappointed 'oh, well' way. Still, look on the bright side: it's not going to kill you to go and have a cup of tea with someone who turns out to be a bit disappointing; and it's going to enhance your life greatly to go and have a cup of tea with someone who turns out to be totally great.

I repeat, for the benefit of older and more sceptical readers: **online is how everyone meets everyone,** these days. It's not weird or sinister or odd or desperate. It's completely normal.

HOW TO BE A FRIEND
TO SOMEONE WHO IS ILL

This is the time of life when many of us first encounter illness in a friend – either because they have something horrible, like cancer, or because they've had a hyster-ectomy, or a hip or knee replacement, or have fallen over (do I sound obsessed with falling over? That's because I am). Some people deal with this better than others, on both sides of the friendship. Here's some advice if you're the healthy one:

- **All of those kind offers are exhausting.** Don't say: 'Shall I cook you something? What would you like? I can do a beef casserole, or would you prefer fish? Or there's that nice tagine I do, you might like that? What about pudding? Should I get some cheese? Now, when are you going to be in?' etc., etc. You'd be amazed at how many people do this. It's really well intentioned, but it means

243

your ill friend has to make a ton of decisions and possibly reorganize her diary. What was meant to be helpful ends up being really effortful and annoying (perhaps even disproportionately so, since the ill friend is unlikely to be in a relaxed, cheerful mood, due to having *quite a lot on her mind*).

- **Just make the food and drop it off in a cool-bag.** Ring the doorbell and hand it over – don't assume the ill friend will be delighted to see you and longing to invite you in for a drink. Don't hover annoyingly as though you're expecting her to. Don't, for God's sake, look wounded when she doesn't. She's ill.

- **Easier still, leave food, posh toiletries, books or whatever tucked away somewhere near the front door,** and send a text to your friend/her husband/ children saying it's there. The husband/ children are the ones to whom you should give reheating information/ use-by dates, etc. – or just stick the instructions on the food itself. Your ill friend does not give a toss about these kinds of minutiae; if you ring her up to explain about oven temperatures, she may see it as you making unreasonable demands on her time.

- **Only offer practical help.** Saying 'How can I help?' once is fine. Ringing every day in a cheerful voice saying 'How can I help?' is irritating and makes you look like an ambulance chaser. Make it very clear to your friend that you're there for her, but don't *nag* her about it. Nor should you make her feel guilty about not taking you up on your kind offer. The wounded tone of voice really has no place here.

- **Too much choice, in this context, is bad.** 'I'll take you out on Saturday' is all that's needed. Your friend doesn't need to share in your entire train of thought about what the afternoon might entail.

- **Ill people tend to be very tired.** Some visits will be spent in companionable silence. That's absolutely fine. Take a book, or some knitting, or some work. But don't play on your phone – it carries with it an unwelcome suggestion of boredom.

- **If your friend falls asleep,** it's fine to have a quick tidy/stick a wash on/ straighten out the kitchen/walk the dog/

get some dinner in. Don't expect any thanks. Your friend is completely caught up in her illness – don't ever make her feel like she has to thank you.

- **If your friend feels awful and gloomy,** allow her to feel awful and gloomy. Don't feel obliged to point out half a dozen positives. It's more helpful to say, 'Yeah, that's completely shit. I'm very sorry.'

- **Don't forget the positives altogether.** Think about them, so they don't sound like platitudes. Sneak them in individually, rather than coming out with a long, implausible list of silver linings. Never lie (white lies are fine). She'll know you're lying, and then she won't trust you. That's not friendship.

- **Don't share miracle cures.** Everyone who's had cancer has heard the one about the fasting and the coffee enemas nine million times. Alternative health is all over the internet these days, and many GPs can advise on complementary therapies. If she wants coffee enemas/a bizarre diet, she'll find them all by herself. Chances are she doesn't, and that you're just getting on her nerves.

- **Don't, for heaven's sake, burst into tears or make a stricken face.** Again, this is incredibly common. It isn't about you and your distress. Never mind if you feel sad/shocked. Now, on top of everything else, your sick friend has to comfort *you*, a person who is well – an absurd situation if ever there was, and one whose absurdity will not be lost on her.

- **Don't pretend you're familiar with her illness.** This is her version of it and her suffering. It's not 'the same' as when your other friend had the same disease, which anyway has a broad variety of outcomes.

- **Be brisk.** Even if you're the most sentimental person in the world, force yourself to be unsentimental. Use your intellect, not your emotions.[2]

- **Don't do competitive caring with your friend's other friends.** You may think it's an expression of love; actually it's an expression of neediness. It's

---

[2] My little daughter has had four serious surgeries. The only way of coping is to put on metaphorical armour. I'm nails when I'm in hospital with her. I'm a tank. It works.

unpleasant for the ill friend to feel that she is caught up in this.

- **See your friend as your friend, and not as a generic ill person.** Don't bring her grapes if she doesn't like grapes, or historical romances if she (the fool) doesn't care for them.

- **Speaking of books: an excellent present is a Kindle,** preloaded with things you think she'd like to read. There is a list of comfort reads in the appendix on page 322.

- **Another excellent present is member- ship of Audible,** a vast online library of talking books.[3]

- **Ill people feel like crap and can be highly conscious of looking like crap.** Turning up with the odd carefully selected (for maximum flatteringness) garment or accessory, whether it's a cardigan or a prosthesis, will be a help.

- **Don't fear jokes,** even if they seem in dubious taste. Whether you're ill or well, it is lovely to laugh.

[3] audible.co.uk

HOW TO BE A FRIEND TO SOMEONE WHO'S UNHAPPY

(NB: Unhappy, not clinically depressed)[4]
There can be quite a lot to be unhappy about at this stage of life: bereavement, divorce or separation, the death of a friend, the death of a career (either through the dawning of retirement or through redundancy).

- **Don't make light of their unhappiness**. Some people can buck up after something has made them very sad, and some people can't. Saying 'Are you *still* upset? It was months ago!' is not helpful.

- **Offer solutions to the unhappiness**. Misery can be oddly seductive; it's quite easy for someone to bat away every helpful suggestion on the grounds that it won't work. Persist.

- **Get them out of the house.** Festering in doom with the curtains half-drawn does not lift anyone's spirits.

[4] If you feel your friend is clinically depressed, the kindest thing you can do is take her to the doctor's.

- **But get them out to do quite an anodyne thing.** If you set up something 'special', you will both feel disappointed if it isn't a success. Go for a coffee and a cake instead.

- **Fresh air is a brilliant medicine:** this sounds ridiculous, but it is nevertheless true. Drag your friend out for a long walk somewhere beautiful.

- **You can't feel unhappy if you're completely distracted.** However, if you're unhappy, even unrelated-seeming things can compound your misery – a painting, a movie, a book, some random article in the newspaper. Pick your distraction carefully, and then distract like mad. Eating is a good one: people rarely say, 'Eating this delicious steak-frites reminds me of how much *he* liked steak.' I mean, everyone likes steak. Do point this out.

- **If the unhappiness is middle-age related** – and realizing that your youth is behind you and your Prime won't last forever can engender feelings akin to panic – gently tell your friend that she is wasting precious time. She could be doing something else, being happy. She owes it to herself to try, at this late stage.

- **After a while, do try the pep talk,** and do try not to make it sound like a lecture. Tell your friend that there are fantastic, brilliant, utterly loveable things about her, and tell her what they are. Tell her that she's in danger of pissing them away. Tell her she gets one life, one shot, and that wallowing in misery like a pig in mud is not a good use of her time.

- **Is she unhappy about things she has no power over** – a bereavement, being dumped by someone, losing her job – or is it more a case of being pissed off with life generally? If it is, it's often fixable. The fat can go on a diet. The thin of hair can get a better haircut. The devastated by wrinkles can get Botox. Rooms can be painted, wardrobes overhauled, friendships mended.

- **Make her laugh.** I am trying really hard not to write that laughter is the best medicine, but I see I've failed.

CHAPTER 8

LIVING WELL

The joys and comforts of domestic bliss

Living well is what you deserve by now. It makes every day a pleasure (and, of course, 'living well is the best revenge', as the poet George Herbert[1] so beadily put it). It is an art, and we should all have mastered it by this point: we're too old to live badly, or haphazardly, or chaotically. It's such a waste. By living well, I don't mean lying on velvet chaises eating, or being fed frosted grapes (though actually I do mean that, too), but rather I mean trying to arrange ordinary things so that enjoyment is everywhere. One of the great pleasures of getting older is finding intense pleasure, delight and contentment in small-to-tiny things: a really good glass of wine, an amazingly comfortable bed,[2] a

---

[1] He also said 'love and a cough cannot be hid'.

[2] Vi-Spring. You've never slept on anything like it – amazing, amazing beds. I said in *The Shops* that getting into a Vi-Spring bed was like 'being supported by the soft hands of the Angelic Host', and I stand by every word.

perfect holiday, a book. A view. The weather. A potter.

THE JOY OF POTTERING

It is *the* joy, really, in some respects, isn't it? Lovely, lovely pottering. Most people love pottering from when they're quite young (toddlers, for instance, love potters). But you can't really get down with the pottering while you still have small children: they don't allow for it. No, true pottering really only comes into its own in middle age and beyond, where people can become actual pottering Olympians: pottering is one of the things that genuinely gets better and better with age, like a cheese.

These years are the golden pottering years – you are entitled to potter now. There's nothing else you especially have to do, and nowhere else you especially have to be. You are FREE TO POTTER. Just pootling about, doing not very much. God, I love it. I *love* it.

The potter is my favourite approach to any event. I potter around the house, I potter about making dinner or hanging

---

Not that many things in life are really worth spending the money on, but beds are an exception. Always get the best bed you can: it is life-changing. Especially now, when you need your rest.

pictures. I potter to the local shops. Pottering means you can always interrupt what you're doing for a nice cup of tea. Pottering means nothing is terribly important, so you can take your time. Pottering doesn't necessarily need a purpose (one of the things I love most about it): I often potter out to the shops, have a potter around them and then potter back, happily empty-handed. If pottering were an art, I'd be Caravaggio.

It's not just the physical act of pottering that I love so dearly, but also things that call pottering to mind. For instance, much of my pottering occurs to a Radio 4 soundtrack. I can also potter about with a book, where I put the book down and pick it up again rather than devouring it in one fell swoop. Some books just are more potterish than others. Gardening can be vigorous, but there's a pottering, dead-heading-here-and-there version, too. Pottering-cooking, where you potter off for supplies, potter back and cook them in a leisurely, pottering way, with the radio on in the background and a glass of wine by your side, is one of my favourite things in the world. Pottering-cooking, followed by leisurely eating, with chats, jokes and interesting discussions, is pretty much why I hate going out. It is *never* as good as a pottery night in.

REDISCOVERING THE JOYS OF NATURE

Some cows in a field. Birds. Nature generally. Of course I understand that there are millions of people who have always loved nature, or birds, or cows, but I wasn't one of them. I thought it was nice enough, Nature, but I didn't make a point of spending as much time as I possibly could gambolling in among it, delirious with joy. Not until we got Brodie.

The Bliss of Dogs

Late middle age is a perfect time to get a dog, provided you feel the demands on your time are manageable and your job doesn't take you away from home – which is why retirement is perfect (as is someone else being at home). Leaving dogs alone at home is cruel and distressing to the dog, and I don't care what anyone says about how they 'get used to it'. They get used to it in the way that a child would also 'get used' to being abandoned for hours every day – except that the child would at least understand that you were coming back. People who leave their dogs at home alone all day are selfish and do not deserve them. A relationship based on abandonment is not a relationship. I could rant for hours about this, but you get the gist.

Anyway, dogs: oh, the joy (assuming you like dogs, of course). I had a dog before, when my sons were very small, and I couldn't do that dog justice at all, I'm sad to say. There was too much going on all the time, and the poor dog was pretty low on the list of priorities. I liked him well enough, and he had a nice time, but to be frank having him was a pain. Dogs need a lot of attention: you have to walk them twice a day, and unless they're very small dogs with very small legs, that takes up a couple of hours at least, regardless of what the weather is doing. Those two hours can be pure pleasure, or they can be pure annoyance, depending on how busy your life is. For me, with grown-up children and a little one at school, they are two hours of absolute bliss (with an added bonus: you get quite fit, with all that walking).

The point is this: a dog will enhance your life in the most extraordinary ways, but only if you can afford the time. If you can't, it will be a pain and everybody, both human and canine, will be sad. People are always going, 'Oh, let's get a dog, dogs are so sweet,' without thinking it through properly. In the early, puppy stages, when they're pooing everywhere and chewing your furniture to shreds, having a dog is not unlike having a new baby – except a species of new baby that doesn't do nappies and has really sharp teeth. So bear this in mind.

But man, dogs are just so *happy*, and that happiness is massively infectious. They just burst with love for everything – grass, leaves, trees, running, dinner, YOU. Unfortunately for me this isn't a manual about having a dog, so I will stop going on now. But if you like dogs, and you've always wanted a dog – and if you have the time for a dog – get a dog. You will not be sorry. You will not be lonely: you will have the best and jolliest companion imaginable. Also, I believe that dog people are really good eggs. The finest eggs, actually. You meet very nice people when you're out and about with your dog and they're out with theirs. Dogs improve every aspect of life, really. They are magic.[3]

Cats are nice, too. You don't run through meadows or along the beach laughing with them, feeling nothing but pure happiness, but that's fine.

A hamster seems to me a tragic sort of pet for an adult, but – whatever floats your boat, I guess. (I am discounting guinea pigs since it occurred to me a couple of years ago that they are basically an enormous head with little paws attached. God bless them and everything, but – it's not right.)

---

[3] It is very important that you research dog breeds properly – never go on looks alone. Retrieving breeds, for instance, are bred to retrieve. It's what they do. They will bug you all day until you give them something to retrieve. Herding breeds are bred to herd, and in the absence of sheep will herd you, your children and your friends. Terriers, my personal favourite, need an enormous amount of exercise (most dogs do). Some breeds are gregarious, some tricksy, some easy-going, some highly strung. Also, *always* buy a dog from a registered breeder. Puppy farms – google them – are an abomination.

SPENDING MONEY

As someone who's recently been sacked by not one but two accountants, I should prefix this by telling you that I am not a good person to take financial advice from. Except, I sort of am, because I'm absolutely brilliant at having a lovely time, and sometimes having a lovely time involves thinking, 'Fuck it. We'll eat pasta, or something,' and stretching your purse strings wide. Here is a list of things that are worth throwing caution to the winds for:

- **Beds,** because you need a comfortable place to rest your old bones (see earlier footnote on page 252).

- **A decent haircut/good colour.**

- **One beautiful, warm winter coat.**

- **A 'good' handbag.** You've earned it by now. Don't start disliking your bag in five years' time – buy something classic that's outside fashion. NB: It should not be too heavy when empty: watch your back. **They're not to every taste** – carried by naff people, much copied – but I really love the classic Louis Vuitton Speedy bags (which are also carried by immaculately chic people, let's not forget). They weigh nothing, you could fit half a house in even the smallest model, they're weather-proof, indestructible and they last forever – mine is my grandmother's. They go with everything, but especially prints. They do look trashy if you're wearing a onesie and Uggs, but the solution is to wear normal clothes in the outside world – plus onesies and Uggs make any bag look trashy, so let's not over-fret. (I love onesies and Uggs.)

- **Comfortable, supportive shoes.** Basically, it isn't so much that you have to buy expensive shoes, but more that you should steer clear of amazingly cheap ones that make your feet go 'splat' (see page 174).

- **Comfortable, correctly fitting underwear.** No need to go mad, but avoid the cheapo sling that gives you the bosom of Matron. If you need supportive underwear, then for goodness' sake buy some. There's no need to slip from nice knickers to granny pants just because your love of comfort now trumps aesthetics. There is, as ever, a happy medium.

- **A DAB radio:** these needn't be expensive either, but given how GREAT radio is, and how entirely conducive to pottering, you might as well invest in a gorgeous leather Roberts.

- **A great big state-of-the-art television:** screen size and HD will help failing eyesight, and you can feel like you're at the cinema from your (great big, super-comfy) sofa.

- **After a certain age, the super-comfy sofa becomes essential,** because you're going to be sitting down a lot and having lots of naps on it. Naps! So refreshing and so great. The bliss of naps! Plus now you can stop feeling guilty about having them in the middle of the day. You're old enough to need them. They're health-naps.

- **Goosedown pillows** – you may prefer those Tempur ones that mould themselves to you (some people swear by them) – **and duvets**. Being idyllically comfortable in the Bed of Joy: priceless.

- **A good laptop.** Cheap ones are a false economy. And if you're going to learn how to have an online life, a good laptop will make everything easier.

- **A mobile phone that you keep updated.** They do useful, life-changing things that your old Motorola from 2006 couldn't dream of.

- **Help where you need it**, if you can afford it. That applies whether the help is with cleaning your home or with getting you up the stairs.

SATISFYING YOUR CULTURAL HUNGER

Cultural hunger becomes more acute in the later years, too, which is why theatres are always packed with older people. I thought this was to do with increased affluence and leisure time – and perhaps the panicky feeling that you just don't know enough – but while those are all certainly true, there's another explanation. A friend of mine, who was perfectly happy to go to the theatre occasionally but never made a particular habit of it, is never away from cultural events these days – three nights a week, on average. I said to her once (because I'm the person who'll suggest meeting for a drink first and then try my hardest to persuade my companion to bunk off culture and go for dinner instead) that I didn't understand why she was consuming culture as if it had a sell-by date.

261

'But it does!' she cried. 'I don't want to miss any landmark event. How many more great Hamlets will there be in our time, *while we're still alive*? I feel compelled to see them all – to book tickets on the off-chance. Which means I have to go to everything, just in case. It's like a compulsion. I can't stop.'

It seems that we have fallow periods, where culture is concerned. The teens and twenties can be periods of full immersion, where you're reading entire Booker shortlists for pleasure and spending your evenings craning your neck from the cheap seats, happy to get even a glimpse of the ballet from behind the giant pillar where you're seated, because you're curious about the world and keen to grow your brain. By your thirties you're looking after children and working, and feeling obliterated. There's no spare money for theatre tickets, even before factoring in the cost of the babysitter, and you don't fancy the restricted-view seats or queuing for returns much any more. It's only in your forties and beyond that you can afford the tickets, that the children are old enough not to require baby-sitters, and that it occurs to you, as my friend said, that you'll probably only see two more great *Traviata*s before you peg it.

Opening New Doors

This cultural hunger – carrying on as though you'd just emerged from a culture famine into a land of cultural plenty – is a kind of displacement activity to do with mortality – quick, quick, see a Vermeer in the flesh, *quick!* – that also crops up in other contexts.

I woke up a few weeks ago in a state of great and genuine sorrow because I would never be an ice skater. This is absurd on any number of levels, really, but let's just take the first one: I have never had any remote interest in ice skating. It has never interested me *in the slightest.* I do not care about ice skating. And yet I really was sad, and the thing that made me sad – it's making me sad again as I type – was the idea that IF I had suddenly decided to love ice skating and to become a competent ice skater, then that could have happened, *in the past.* The world was my ice-skating oyster, if I wished it to be so. That's no longer true. I mean, yes, I could learn to skate competently – and even well, I suppose – if I put my mind to it. But I would be me, now, tragi-comically. I would never be a nineteen-year-old ice skater, twirling on the ice, hair flying. When it comes to ice skating, I have absolutely missed the boat. It's gone. It's a door that's shut.

I don't feel this about all sorts of things, as this book demonstrates – not about love, or relation-ships, or any of the real nitty-gritty. But I feel it about closed possibilities when it comes to *actions.* For instance, I find it extremely disconcerting that I'll probably never go to China now, realistically. I've always thought I'd go to China. I can *picture* myself in China, milling about, eating dim sum; I can even picture a road with a chicken walking across it and some low-slung buildings to the left. (I thought this was a beautiful sort of dream-memory, or a powerful photograph from years ago, but now I'm thinking my point of reference might be *Kung Fu Panda*.) I am going to have to make an effort and get myself to China before it's too late and I'm too old, but it's not an effort I especially *want* to make because I have also never been to Japan[4] or Australia (which sounds jollier). There's a list in my head of things I've never done or seen, places I've never been, and next to that list there's a clock, ticking quite loudly. It makes me feel a bit like hyperventilating.

Conversational Russian! A butchery course! Climbing Kilimanjaro! My US road trip! My archaeology degree at the University of the Highlands and Islands! It doesn't only apply to culture and travel, either, which is why people in their fifties often start reading the classics voraciously – last summer, I knew three people who were determinedly planning on 'doing Proust' over their holidays – or starting to learn a new language. (This is a very, very good thing to do brain-wise, like a sort of mega version of doing crosswords – says me, who can't even get her arse in gear to learn conversational Russian.) A University of Edinburgh study in 2014, published in the *Annals of Neurology*, found that reading, verbal fluency and intelligence

---

[4] Mind you, if one judged a culture on its pornography, one would not fancy Japan much.

were improved in a study of 262 people tested either aged eleven or in their seventies. A previous study had suggested that being bilingual could delay the onset of dementia by several years. It's at least got to be worth a shot.[5]

Emoting Wildly

Another thing that happens culture-wise is what may, at first sight, look like the dropping away of one's critical faculties: we are keen to be pleased, and we find ourselves pleased, or delighted, or transported more often than we did in our youth, when our default position may have been cynicism. Now, we want to like stuff and we want to applaud, and that is because we have an intense appreciation of, and admiration for, human endeavour. We are thrilled and amazed by the achievements of human beings. There is so much to find affecting. There is so much to *feel*. These days I am moved, sometimes to tears, by the fact that the orchestra even *exists*: all those little humans, doing their beautiful art together. I also experience it with brushstrokes on paintings. I am in tears at the pathetic, beautiful human-ness of it: the marks of the actual little brush hairs that the painter dipped in his paint. O noble painter! O noble brush! It's unbearable.

[5] The University of the Third Age is absolutely brilliant and operates nationwide and online. It is completely free. See u3a.org.uk.

In middle age and beyond, we are increasingly susceptible to the poignancy and transience of human effort. It's why some of us, who would have stared in utter and genuine bafflement at someone who cried at the opera – never mind at the telly – spend half our time in tears at funny little things from everyday life, as well as at art whose purpose is to move.

I find gardening very moving, too. All that hope, all that nurturing and cherishing and *care*, for one little plant, and then the plant stands with its fellow plants – a band of brothers – and together they make something dazzling. And the sea! Mighty and eternal, with its relentless tides, while people are born and die and kingdoms crumble to dust. I mean, floods of tears. But the sea always also makes me feel like having sex, so that's cheerier.[6]

CHANGING FACULTIES, CHANGING POLITICS

Not the full U-turn, you understand. But a change starts to occur in late middle age, and it's a disconcerting one: we start feeling genuine anger towards the people and things that try to spoil our time. Antisocial behaviour is our bugbear: vandalism, graffiti, litter, noise nuisance,

[6] Also thunderstorms. Anything dramatically elemental. Intimations of mortality, innit.

dog poo, animal cruelty. Of course all of these things have been around for a long time, but I never used to notice them. If you asked me at the age of twenty-five about noise nuisance, I'd tell you that my neighbours just needed to chill – the party stopped at 3 a.m., which means they had all weekend to sleep in. At thirty-five, I'd have some anecdote about a car alarm that wouldn't turn off. But ask me now and I have a catalogue of daily grievances (for starters, I had to *leave home* to write some of this book, such is the bleedin' racket right outside my front door).

And another thing: litter. Obviously, nobody likes litter. Nobody, no matter how young they are, goes, 'Yay, the park is covered in trash, what good news.' At our age, though, that dislike turns into some-thing else – a *very strong feeling* that is, in my case, akin to an obsession. People who don't pick up their dog poo – or, even worse, pick it up and hang the bag from a tree – fall into the same category. (I chase them, like a mad bat, going, 'Hello? HELLO? Excuse me? You left a poo.') People who won't do their jobs properly: same thing. (You are being paid to take my order; it's forgivable to bring me the wrong food, but don't roll your eyes when I point it out. You are being paid to take my coffee order; please don't stand around excavating your nostrils instead.)

This can leach into what may feel, depending on where you started, like a sudden lurch rightwards politically. For example, you – who have always been generally liberal and left-leaning – find yourself thinking, 'This Tory over here is saying quite a nuanced and intelligent thing, and I agree with him. In fact, I'd vote for that policy. How odd.' Politics can become confusing in middle age. I don't mean that we start giving UKIP the glad eye, or start spouting nonsense about immigrants (the people who spout about immigrants almost always live in rural areas where there aren't any, which is either hilarious or tragic, or perhaps both). But some things really start bugging us now, and they are often things we really didn't much think about before we hit our Prime. These days, we screw in our monocles, like so many retired brigadiers. We harrumph. We really mind.

Anyway, some words of comfort: it seems to me that you are not, in fact, turning into the *Daily Mail*, because left and right meet over these issues – noise, litter, nuisance, antisocial behaviour, an apparent falling away of kindness, an increase in rudeness. Anything that spoils our own immediate environment affects all of humanity. These are universal concerns: everybody cares about them, regardless of their politics. You have not turned right so much as found a commonality with people that you didn't know you shared, and that's not a bad thing, in the end.

Rediscovering Hobbies

Hobbies needn't have anything to do with culture, of course. My main hobby is cooking, which is just as well as I live in a house with people who have abnormal, gargantuan appetites – but who, crucially, are able to feed themselves, these days. So my cooking is now a pleasure, rather than a chore (or if not quite a chore, then certainly a task to be ticked off the long daily list). By the way, if you can't cook, or are – still – a bad cook, it's never too late to learn. Being able to feed yourself and your loved ones delicious things is a very, very nice thing to be able to do. There's a list of excellent cookbooks in Appendix 3.

My other hobby, along similar lines, is houses – or rather, my house. My *home*. Making sure it looked nice used to mean 'making sure it didn't look completely trashed'. Now it means feeling disproportionate pleasure at finding a really lovely teapot at a car boot sale (hobby number two) or rummaging in a junk shop (three). All of these hobbies can now be indulged, rather than crammed into an already over-packed week. Doing the things that you want to do, and having the time to do them in, is just the most fantastic treat – as, of course, is having the time to do nothing at all.

Sometimes I look back at the time, many aeons ago, when we all admired people who did things incredibly fast – a woman would pop out a baby and be back at work the next day, expected to be 'Superwoman' in her juggling. How silly. What a waste of life, not to sit still and enjoy things properly. What a pity that, instead of slowly examining things from all angles, taking pleasure from each one, we should have spent decades believing that speed was best, that bashing stuff out pronto, asap – 'I need it by yesterday' – was any way to live. This realization is another one of the nicest things about getting older.

Slowing Down without Stagnating

Don't rest on your slow laurels, though. The thing that very old people always say when you ask them is that they can't stand not feeling useful, of service to either individuals or society – I know an eighty-year-old lady who twice a week goes off on her rounds to read to 'the old people'. Again and again, this feeling of purposelessness is identified as the moment where the rot sets in and the decline starts, especially among those old people who are also lonely through losing their spouse.

It is really important to keep feeling that you are

useful, that you contribute – and even that you are giving something back. This may take the form of charity work or volunteer work, or it may just translate into helping those close to you. Whatever: it's important to do it. Unless you have unusually high feelings of self-worth, you do to a certain extent measure yourself by what you contribute, in a small way, to the world at large, to your community, to your household. Age needn't be a barrier to that.

MOVING HOUSE OR DOWNSIZING

For many people, round about now is the time you wonder whether you might like to move house – either because you're downsizing, or because you never really meant to live where you are forever. Now that schools – and perhaps work – are out of the way, well, if you're lucky, your options may become wider. It is not a decision to be entered into lightly, but it's worth really thinking about how and where you want to spend your Prime and post-Prime. Instead of hunkering down and waiting for life to gradually grind to a halt, moving house can feel like setting off on an adventure.

Of course, there are dozens of other fantastic ways of keeping things new and fresh – ones that don't involve bricks and mortar – and besides, you may delight in the old, the familiar and the comfortable. It's possible to do both, though: experience the delight *and* the adventure. But I do think that there is something almost dizzying about the idea of suddenly being able to live exactly where you like, purely because you like it. Not because the schools are good, or because it's handy for the commute, or because it was all you could afford ten, twenty or thirty years ago – or because living on the edge of a cliff staring out at the wild Atlantic is, well, not *practical*. For now, right now, in this window alone, it may be that nobody cares about practical any more, and that's a thrilling thing.

Seizing the Day

This window of not caring about any of the ordinary niceties is not huge, I should add. At some point – hopefully at some point in the far and distant future – you will not be able to live on the edge of a cliff, because boring practicalities will come into play once again: what if you slip and fall off the cliff (though it beats dying of boredom in a nursing home, if you ask me)? What about proximity to doctors and hospitals? And so on. Before all that, though, there may, if you are very lucky, be time for carefreeness – the carefreeness that was a given when people had children young, as I was saying on page 199. Maybe the stars are aligned: your parents are either hale and hearty or no longer with us; your children are adults; you can work from home, or from home for most of the week. You may be retired, or thinking about it. Or you may be reading this and thinking, 'Oh! I want that to be me, eventually.' Well, start planning.

What a gift, to be carefree now. It's like the Second Coming. We all thought that our one period of carefreeness was in childhood – but that wasn't really true. Childhood, especially late childhood, is beset with anxieties: who am I, what shall I become, what shall I do, how shall I be, what will become of me? In middle age and upwards, you know the answer to all of those things. You've done your decades at the coalface and now . . . now you really *are* free.

GET ON WITH IT, I say. Of course there are lots of variables, mostly to do with dependants of all kinds. But even if you feel like you're very far away from that cliff-top house, even if you feel that you are still problematically tied down, it is still true that you are freer than you were. Because now, when your time isn't other people's, it is emphatically your own. What do I mean by this? Well, when you had little children, say, there were times in the day when your time was yours – snatched moments here and there in which you were, technically, free to do with your time as you saw fit. In reality, the background noise was omnipresent, and it was impossible to wholly tune it out. So you'd be having a 'relaxing' bath, but going through a mental checklist in your head: 'Food shop, gym kit, swimming stuff, playdate, must pick up dry cleaning, what's for supper tomorrow, nits, not sure about that new friend Billy made, piano

. . .' And on, and on, it went: 'Must check on Mum, must talk to doctor about beta blockers. Oh – appointment with dentist for Molly, which reminds me, nothing for the packed lunch. When are we seeing the Smiths, is it Thursday? Where's my black dress? I haven't see it for ages.' On, and on, and on, and on.

I don't have these thought processes any more, at forty-eight. My dad's dead, my mum's A-OK, my stepfather has a wife, my siblings are doing great, two of my children are adults and the third is thriving, the people I love are healthy and well. There is loads of crap (small crap – droppings rather than pats) lobbed into my day on a regular basis, because that's what life is like, but never mind them. And there are some anxieties too, of course, because I am a human being – but being a human being of middle age, a) there are fewer and b) I really, really don't sweat the small stuff. And so, by and large, I feel freer and more *free of cares* than I did at eighteen or at any time since.

SHOULD YOU DOWNSIZE/MOVE AWAY?

I have a constant internal dialogue going on about this with myself. Most unexpectedly, it originates with my newfound fixation with the natural world – I, who used to think that there was literally nothing duller than nature, and who now spends large chunks of her day pining for the country-side. It's almost like a visceral need: I'm constantly walking down some sweaty London street and thinking, 'This is not right. Where is the GREEN? Where is the WATER?' It's been going on for years now, so I know it's not a passing fancy, just as I know that at some point I'm going to have to do something about it – a prospect I find deeply exciting. It's one of my top three things about getting older. Until then, there's property porn.

Unless you are planning to turn your too-big home into an OAP commune, as per page 112, then yes, you probably should downsize. Another strange thing that comes with age is the realization that change is no longer scary, even if you've been a person whose defining character-istic has traditionally been 'not good with change'. Now, though, change becomes your friend. Time is running out: why not shake things up a bit, just because you can? I don't think it's any accident that so many elderly people end up at the seaside, for instance: they've probably wanted to live by the sea for the past forty years. Now that they're able to, why wouldn't they? Why wouldn't I, and why wouldn't you?

Having said all of that, rather breezily, sometimes I feel almost panicked by the idea of, effectively, leaving home again, thirty years after I did it for the first time. But I've thought and thought about it, and the only thing I would miss is the easy-peasy access to food from a zillion different countries. I wouldn't miss my friends, because they would come and stay. I wouldn't miss 'culture' in an unmanageable way: I love the idea of getting on the train specifically to inspect a new exhibition at the British Museum. I wouldn't miss the shops – the dear, dear shops – because, rather incredibly, really, in the twenty-first century the shops are no longer about bricks and mortar. I could wear what I am wearing now, furnish my house with the exact same things, buy people the same presents as I do now – all through the mind-blowing magic (and it really is, isn't it? We don't stop often enough to acknowledge the magic) of the internet. So really, it's just the food. Happily, I love cooking. Peculiar ingredients are all available online, too.[7]

Still, this is the internal monologue that runs through my head every day:

- **I'm from the city.** I've lived in the city all my life. I love the city – and actually,

---

[7] I find Sous Chef (souschef.co.uk) particularly helpful.

in very many respects, the city has shaped who I am. I love the easy access to culture, I love the way I can eat amazing food from a hundred different countries, I love the people – broad-minded and liberal. I love the excitement and the noise. I love everything. It's home.

- **I get out of town as often as I can.** It's like a joke. I used to spend my money on clothes or going out; now I spend every spare penny on weekend cottages. At the beginning I used to laugh and think I'd snap out of it, but it's been five years now. Nearly six. This has got to be telling me something. But see my previous point.

- **Of course liberal, broad-minded people are also found outside cities.** However, having been to dinner parties in the deepest shires, their existence is not necessarily immediately obvious.

- **I count black and brown people when I am outside a city.** Thin pickings, let's say. For what it's worth, this is my main obstacle. I can't live anywhere where people might describe me – or worse still, my children – as 'exotic'. ('But where are you *really* from?' Note to those people: no, we don't consider it a compliment, actually. It's the racial equivalent of 'artistic' for 'gay' – and belongs in 1973, tops. City-dwellers know this.)

- **BUT OH MY GOD, THE COUNTRY-SIDE IS SO BEAUTIFUL.** It speaks straight to my heart. I could walk the dog along a beach every morning, or through marshland, or through a fat, lush green field (if the field were mine. Otherwise my dog would be shot. Country ways for country people. Am I a country person? All the evidence says no. And yet . . .).

- **The people are so friendly.** This or that village is so gorgeously pretty. It has a butcher's! A fishmonger's! A fruit and veg shop! The pub does brilliant food and there's a huge roaring fire in winter. The cinema's only thirty miles away.

- **[Back to earth] thirty miles!** In London I can walk to two different ones in ten minutes.

- **But I never go to the cinema.** I wait and watch everything on DVD or TV.

This is a sign, right? It's a sign from God to move to the country. And the culture thing – when was the last time I willingly took myself to an exhibition or a play? Sure, the restaurant thing is true. But I can cook. I can cook most things, from most countries, and if I can't I'm willing to learn. I'm not going to perish for want of ham croquetas, or Pakistani food, or ceviche.

- **I'm also a lot better with insects and rodents than I used to be.** We'll never be pals, but I no longer check out and into a B&B until someone has removed them. This may also be a sign from God.

- **But my friends!** I love my friends, who are all in the city. I would perish without them. Who would come to dinner? Who would we hang out with?

- **Our friends could come and stay.** And we're really happy hanging out on our own, me and my beloved.[8] That's quite

[8] Perhaps before we kick the bucket someone will have invented a word for the person you live and sleep with that isn't 'boyfriend' (we're not fifteen) or 'partner' (we are not a law firm or a same-sex couple). Partner (though I do sometimes use this word myself)! Ugh.

a rare thing, isn't it? We should just hang out on our own, on our beach/in our field, delirious with clam-like joy. He could work upstairs. I could work from the kitchen table, as is my wont. Then we'd meet for lunch.

- **But we wouldn't have been anywhere or seen anybody.** We'd have no news for each other.

- **But who cares about stupid news?** We'd have read books, and seen interesting things on walks – much more interesting to talk about than what Stupid said to Bum.

- **And anyway, we'd make new friends.** We do actually know how.

- **Yeah, but . . . country friends.** They're never going to know us like our *real* friends know us.

- **Man, look at the sky.** So much sky. All this fresh air. This beautiful sky and fresh air, and this beautiful cottage right over here that I am not at all furnishing in my head – dear me, no (we'd have to get anther sofa).

- **MONEY.** A city shoebox equals a spacious cottage in the country.

- **But I'm from the city.** I've lived in the city all my life . . . [REPEAT, ad nauseam].

NB: If this sounds familiar, the most sensible solution may be to leave the city for a small market town or a big village. Or for another city, but one that's smaller and, say, coastal. The culture shock shouldn't be overwhelming, there would still be great coffee and great restaurants that you could walk to, and all would be well.[9]

Or you could just bite the bullet. You only live once, as the young people say.

GROWING OLD 'DISGRACEFULLY'

To me, this is rather an antiquated notion, as if there were only two ways of being and two ways of doing things: sweet old apple-cheeked nana in the zip-up bootees over here, bustling about making cups of tea; and – what? – 'sharper' old

---

[9] I am writing this chapter in Norfolk. I've just interrupted myself because I noticed a toad waddling about outside and I needed to get a good look at it. I took its picture with my phone and then I moved it off the path. See? I'm not the person I used to be.

nana over here, with cheekbones maybe, drinking espresso and being 'a character'? Being 'a character' is my idea of hell – 'Hello, I think you'll find *I'm a bit of a character.*' I mean, please, let's all just die right now instead.

The woman – Jenny Joseph – who wrote that poem about being old and wearing purple ('When I am an old woman I shall wear purple / With a red hat which doesn't go, and doesn't suit me') has a lot to answer for. Interestingly, she wrote it in 1961. I thought it was a more-or-less modern poem, but I hadn't even been born in 1961 – which is funny, because I know the poem by heart and it's still how I define, to myself, a certain version of ageing. It works as shorthand for eccentric, self-pleasing, a bit naughty, perhaps even 'outrageous'. Actually the poem is completely antiquated – 'Do wear purple,' you want to say to Jenny Joseph. 'Wear purple ass-less chaps, for all we care.' But it does just go to show how stuck we are with this notion: say 'old woman' and we think of a poem written over fifty years ago as the only antidote to the granny-at-the-Aga image.[10] Why do I even *know* the poem? Why would I pay it any attention? It would be like living in 1961 and

---

[10] Plus, the old woman in the poem is wearing WHACKY. Nightmare, right there. Marginally preferable, I suppose, to 'When I am an old woman I shall wear Issey Miyake pleats / And a grey bob which doesn't suit me . . .' But not by much.

taking advice on how to comport yourself from an Edwardian poet.

Having said all of that, you may want to bear in mind that popping your clogs while doing something injudicious and thrilling – and it would have to be a great deal more thrilling than wearing stupid purple – is a fine way to go, and may save you from a long, slow, agonizing decline in a grim little room that smells faintly of pee. There's a lot to be said for living dangerously. As the smackhead grandpa says to his grandson in *Little Miss Sunshine*: 'When you're young, you're crazy to do that shit. You get to be my age, you're crazy not to do it.' (Please don't take this too literally. I am not exhorting you to try heroin. If you've always wanted to try weed while sitting in a teepee, though, now's probably not a bad time.)

There is no need to grow old in any declared style, 'disgracefully' or otherwise. You know what you like doing, and what makes you happy: do more of it. You know what gets you down: do less of that; aim to get it down to zero. All you can be is who you are: the version of yourself that is the most pleasing to you and that makes you the happiest, living the best (in all senses) life that you can, in a place (hopefully) that you love, doing things you love doing, with people (and maybe animals) you love in your life.

CHAPTER 9

THE MENOPAUSE

Don't panic. It's going to be fine. Read on . . .

(A plea: please read this chapter even if you're years away from the ol' meno. It contains things you can do NOW to maybe help yourself later.)

I am a reasonably intelligent, well-educated woman who interests herself in the world around her, in people, in news – both medical and otherwise – and in her own body. And yet here is what I knew about the menopause before I started writing this book: a) it happens to everyone female,[1] b) it's awful, and therefore c) we shan't talk about it because it's too much of a downer. It is simply *extraordinary*, this lack of – and fear of – accessible knowledge: there are no other situations in which it applies. There is no other topic that relates to our own intimate lives that makes us cover our ears. Also extraordinary is our collective unwillingness to discuss something that is

---

[1] Born female, I should say.

284

JUST AROUND THE CORNER for so many of us, and for every woman, eventually.

If the topic does come up, the conversation can be précised into 'dunno', 'woe' and 'ugh' before it moves on to something jollier. The menopause is truly the last taboo: we're delighted to show how modern we are by talking loudly and in detail about sex, sexual partners, sexual quirks, periods, and every bodily function, fluid or emission imaginable – but when it comes to The Withering, there is only crashing silence. It's not sexy. It's the opposite of sexy – the end of fecundity, the beginning of nan-dom – and so we don't want to know. This is a fantastically silly stance to adopt, for any number of reasons, including the fact that being a sort of collective village idiot on the subject is really not sexy either. Also, **what is the point of being proud of being a woman if you're going to be desperately ashamed** of this one bit of it – this last third of your actual life?

UNDERSTANDING OUR HORMONES

The whole question of women's hormones and the way they're never discussed is just as odd. Recently a male friend (aged fifty!) said to me that he didn't know a single man, himself included, who knew *anything* about women and their hormones – only the lame old joke about periods and being in a bad mood. 'Now I think about it, it seems completely bizarre,' he said, 'especially given that we all come from a woman's body.' And he's not wrong: men having even a rudimentary understanding of the way our hormones work would probably save thousands of arguments – and perhaps even relationships – a week.

Women often don't understand their own hormones properly, either. Or at least, I don't – or didn't. I got the vague gist, in that I knew the names, but I couldn't have broken it down for you. And yet it's such a good idea to understand what's going on with them, and to understand the effects they may have on your body and mind, not least because understanding means that you can keep your partner and children informed of the fact that you are behaving in X way because of Y reason. If you do this, they'll have an idea of what's going on and will hopefully be supportive. If you don't, you run the risk of having your kids rolling their eyes behind your back and mouthing, 'She's gone completely mad,' at each other (as I fear many of us did with our own mothers). So here we go. Here are the hormones that concern us most in this chapter:

* **Oestrogen** is basically the main sex female hormone – as in sexual characteristics and sexual matters, not as in shagging. It grows your bosoms and genitals at puberty and governs menstruation, among other things. It also protects your heart and bones. It has a finger in every pie, oestrogen, and its petering

out has wide-ranging consequences and result in a wide variety of symptoms.

* **Progesterone** is produced in the ovaries and is pretty much the pregnancy hormone. Before you have your period, it thickens the womb lining in preparation for an egg to be implanted; if no egg is implanted, you menstruate. Progesterone levels rise in pregnancy (when it is also produced by the placenta) – in order to keep you pregnant, basically. When you have finished a pregnancy, progesterone levels drop off sharply, and this can sometimes cause post-natal depression. They also drop significantly after the menopause.

* **Testosterone** is not just for men, though they produce more of it.[2] It is the sex (as in shagging) hormone in that it affects your sex drive and, for instance, ease of orgasm, among other things. It also has a bearing on bone strength and muscle density. Testosterone is also involved with collagen production (collagen is what keeps your skin plumped and smooth). Most women continue to make an adequate amount of testosterone after menopause, which

---

[2] The male menopause, such as it is, has to do with falling levels of testosterone and is called the andropause. I am writing this so that I can tell you its other name, which is hypogonadism.

means that most women's libido is unaffected (and may even become turbo-charged, which I'll get to later in this chapter). However, this is not the case where a woman has had early menopause, or menopause brought on by surgery, radiation or chemotherapy. It's OK, though: even then, there are loads of things you can do.

There are other hormones to do with all of this stuff; for simplicity, let's just stick to the fact that they are mostly produced in the pituitary gland (it's the size of a pea and it lives in your brain). Now, not everyone is affected by their hormones in the same way, which is how you get some women who barely notice they're having a period and other women who are in physical discomfort and emotional turmoil every month.

WHAT IS THE MENOPAUSE?

It's the time when your periods stop and don't come back. If you haven't had a period for two years, you have gone through the menopause. Welcome, greybeard!

This is how it happens: your ovaries stop being able to produce oestrogen and progesterone. This happens when they (the ovaries) have not many egg cells left – you are born with all your egg cells, rather amazingly, and they start reducing from puberty. (Actually, they start reducing in tiny increments from the moment you pop out of the womb.) The number dwindles further during your twenties and thirties, and then starts seriously falling from the age of forty onwards. Imagine a giant tin of caviar, packed to the brim: that's how you are, head down the birth canal, ready to be born. By the time you're a teenager, someone's been at the tin with a teaspoon. They're using a normal spoon in your twenties, a dessert spoon in your thirties and a jumbo ladle in your forties. By the time you're in your fifties, the tin's pretty much empty: there are only a few weensy bits of caviar clinging to the inside of the lid. I've slightly put myself off delicious caviar with this analogy, but never mind. When the egg cells start being thin on the ground, your ovaries, which have until now been responding in a hearty and vivacious way to hormones from your pituitary gland, now become less good at doing so: their Mexican wave becomes a weak raised finger. This matters because the pituitary hormones were prompting your ovaries to make FSH, follicle stimulating hormone (which among other things directs the reproductive process), and its sidekick LH, luteinizing hormone, which a) triggers ovulation and b) stimulates production of testosterone. Still with me? So, because of all this, your ovaries are no longer producing much oestrogen. And this, broadly, is why menopause occurs.

The average age for menopause in the UK is fifty-one, but it can happen much earlier or much later (I have a friend who's fifty-nine and still has normal periods). If it happens before you're forty-five, it's called 'early' menopause, and it's called 'premature' menopause if it happens before the age of forty. By the age of fifty-four, 80 per cent of women have stopped having periods.

WHAT IS PERIMENOPAUSE?

It's the years leading up to the menopause, when you may feel perfectly well and not notice anything problematic afoot at all. But you will still eventually notice that your periods are becoming irregular, erratic, or few and far between. (Confusingly, it's possible to not have periods for several months and then for them to come back as normal for a while. Do not stop using contraception.) Your levels of oestrogen and progesterone will be changing; you may or may not experience symptoms such as hot flushes, night sweats, insomnia and (hurrah) vaginal dryness and its pal, urinary trouble. These last two occur because of lack of oestrogen, ditto bladder infections and weeing a bit when you laugh (God help us), especially if you have had multiple vaginal births – though, as I cannot emphasize enough, NONE OF THESE IS A GIVEN, and there are plenty of effective solutions.

Then there are headaches, mood swings and loss of libido, plus, wahoo, there's possibly the start of osteoporosis – this basically means that your bones get thin and weak, making them a) more breakable and b) liable to make you lose height. Those shrunken old ladies you see: that's osteoporosis (and scoliosis, curvature of the spine, sometimes). We'll be going through all of these things individually below. Please note also: you may not have many, or indeed any, of these symptoms. My own GP says that only 10 to 15 per cent of his middle-aged female clients come to him for help to do with menopausal issues. The rest just stop having periods and get on with it, only very mildly inconvenienced; he says that these women often make one lone appointment to say, 'My periods have stopped but I don't seem to have all the symptoms I was expecting. Is something wrong?' Nothing is wrong, of course: we are just conditioned – because the whole topic of the menopause is so stupidly under-discussed – to expect the worst. **Thirty per cent of British women go through the menopause with no unmanageably dramatic symptoms at all.**[3]

Where the symptoms – or some of them – do occur, they will do so when you are perimenopausal, but they may become more intense with the onset of the actual menopause. Some women experience the symptoms for a brief period of time, and some experience them for years.[4] And

[3] This figure is from the Menopause Matters website (menopausematters.co.uk).

[4] At a reading I did recently, a woman in the audience

some, of course, barely experience them at all (she said, clutching her straw tightly in her fevered hand). Also, you can – and probably will – experience the symptoms every now and then, rather than constantly.

THE ROLE OF DIET AND EXERCISE

Before I go into detailed specifics, here's an important thing: you will have noticed that the words 'bone' and 'muscle' keep cropping up. Both bone and muscle density (where dense = good) are governed by the hormones that are, as we speak, falling away like tragic petals. It does not, therefore, take Holmesian powers of deduction to work out that, in an ideal world, you want your bones and muscles to be in top nick before you enter the perimenopausal stage, let alone the full-blown menopause. We are talking about two obvious and basic things here that we can all do something about: diet and exercise. They are not 100 per cent guarantors of an easy menopause, by any means. But my goodness – it's not going to hurt, is it? Therefore, **it is vitally important to eat properly**.

As I have said throughout this book, we are too

announced that she has been going through the menopause for *seventeen years*. There was pin-drop silence while the whole audience – 98 per cent women – stared at each other, ashen, with absolute horror.

old to be on permanent faddy diets, too old to skip meals, too old to be one of those women who basically walks around not knowing she has malnutrition because she only eats kale and chia seeds. You may be pleased that you're fifty-five and a size 0: you've every right to be pleased and to thank your metabolism if that happens naturally. But you'd be insane to be pleased if the price has been starving yourself and/or exercising brutally and obsessively for years or decades, or barely looking after yourself and eating crap. You shouldn't be pleased; you should be properly worried and taking remedial measures right now, because you won't be feeling pleased, or carefree and rock 'n' roll, when you're suddenly four foot six and piteously frail. Equally, of course, you'd be insane to think that being clinically obese and flabby-limbed is a good idea at this time of life (or ever, frankly).

Concerning eating crap, briefly: I worry terribly about the calamitous-seeming consequences of ingesting the antibiotics in the meat we eat. If this sounds like me being a hippie, it's really not: I am always on the side of science, and I happen to be wildly carnivorous. But looking into hormones generally, and their effects on us when ingested, led me into all sorts of directions, and – yeesh. Also, all the notably unhippieish, pinstriped and august medics I spoke to had strong views on this, and none of them were cheery. I'm digressing, but my advice is, eat organic meat – grass-fed, if it's beef. (If that means you can only afford it once a week: good. A roast chicken on Sunday, as a treat, is the way to go.)

Diet

I happen to think that government healthy-eating guidelines are nuts in some places (those places being an acceptance of pointless empty carbohydrates). The 'five a day' advice is fine provided you err on the side of vegetables, since fruit is just as likely as sweets to rot your teeth: sugar is sugar, even when it's fructose, and fruit acids can be very unkind to enamel. Simple carbohydrates (white stodgy things, basically) do nothing aside from causing your blood sugar levels to crash and making you sluggish and fat. Pasta and bread can be divine, but not every day (unless you are an athlete, and even then . . .). I am also of the opinion that 'diet' anything is evil and will eventually make you sick, that artificial sweeteners are dodgy in the extreme, that sugar in all its forms is unbelievably bad for you, and that good fats (butter, olive and nut oils) are your friends.[5]

I think that calories are largely irrelevant. I believe in clean, honest, un-manipulated food that is recognizably food. Put very briefly: if I want to

[5] For heaps more on this, and an in-depth explanation of why I think these things, see *Neris and India's Idiot-Proof Diet*, also published by Fig Tree/Penguin.

be at an optimal weight – and it's a consideration here (many menopausal women traditionally put on weight due to hormonal changes, and it all goes around the middle, in that insecty way I was mentioning on page 180) – and if I want to feel physically well and strong, I base my diet around a little protein, a lot of good fats and vegetables, the leafier and greener the better, and I drink clean spirits rather than sugary wines. Not always – you'd die of boredom – but *mostly*. Speaking of drinking: stay hydrated. Keep drinking plenty of water.

I am not a medic or nutritionist, of course, but nor am I saying any of this off the top of my head because I feel like it: I spent a year researching this stuff and consulted several professionals before reaching the above conclusion in the course of writing a previous book. My point is: eat well. If you don't know how to eat well – and if you mistrust my advice – ask a doctor or nutritionist. Buy the best food you can possibly afford, and *love* what you eat. Do not be neurotic about food: it's never not tiresome, and at this particular age it might actually do you terrible harm. Good nutrition will show in your skin and hair – both of which are liable to suffer the effects of decreased collagen production – as well as on your body, inside and out.

Exercise

Keep your muscles strong. I'd start ranting on about the brilliance of yoga here if I hadn't ranted more than enough already, but – well, you know my views by now (OK, one last time: yoga is *all* about strength and flexibility, which is exactly what you want here). Otherwise, moderate cardiovascular exercise, also known as aerobic exercise, is the key. This means not a frenetic Zumba class, but a brisk longish walk that causes you to break into a sweat. It means not fanatically pounding along pavements, but swimming or cycling: exercise that gets you a little out of breath. Not only is aerobic exercise good for your heart but the type of resistance-exercise that has your muscles pulling on your bones is good for maintaining bone density.

IS MENOPAUSE THE SAME FOR EVERYONE?

No, it is not, as we have seen. It can drag on and on – seemingly interminably – or it can whizz by in a (hot) flash, or it can (most often) be something in between. Some women wake up with the sheets drenched, while some women lightly perspire in a wholly manageable way.

If Not, Why Not?

The chances are that your experience of the menopause will closely mirror your mother's. Ask her (and try not to be annoyed when she is irritatingly vague about remembering the specifics). Most women are 'done' within two to five years. Nobody yet knows why women are affected in such wildly varying ways.

Is It Possible to Have Been through the Menopause and Not Noticed?

I'd like to say yes, but you'd really have to be terribly unobservant. Nobody has zero symptoms, but some women do go through the whole thing with only very minor manifestations, and feel that they can easily take these in their stride.

'When I was too hot, I kicked off the duvet or opened a window,' a friend says. 'That was it.'

Another friend says, 'My best advice re hot flushes is to stay perfectly still when they happen. Don't budge – even the smallest movement makes you feel hotter. They pass very quickly. Also, what draws attention to them is melodramatic self-fanning, removing all your layers and going "hoo-hoo".'

A third friend found that, far from going off sex, she was very frisky at all times – and this is a medically recognized thing. It's to do with a surge in testosterone, which more or less stays put while your other hormones fall away. 'I'm having the best sex I've ever had,' more than one woman told me in the course of researching this book.

Before I start on my Q&A: *if* you have symptoms that really bother you, do consider going to a gynaecologist rather than just your GP. GPs' knowledge varies; gynaecologists are specialists in this field

What Is a Hot Flush? What Is Happening?

The immediate cause of hot flushes is dilation of the blood vessels in the skin, though the precise reason why they should be a feature of the menopause is unclear. The current theory is that they are induced by the effects of the decline in oestrogen levels on the functioning of the hypothalamus in the brain, which is also involved in regulating the internal core temperature of the body.

What Causes Night Sweats?

Nobody is absolutely sure – but they're nocturnal hot flushes, basically.

Will I Have Vaginal Dryness or Vaginal Atrophy?

Probably not, but it's possible. Neither of these – caused by lack of frickin' oestrogen, AGAIN – is on anybody's wish list. (Vaginal atrophy is the thinning and drying of the vaginal walls, which makes sex painful.) There is some evidence that regular sex, either with somebody or with yourself, can be helpful at keeping things boingy and elastic. First port of call, if not: lube, and plenty of it. We all know where the chemist is, though I am of the opinion that the lubiest lubes are to be found in reputable sex emporia. This hardly seems the time or the place, but I'll say it anyway: a super-slippy lube that is designed specifically for bumming is a great deal lubier than a common or garden lube from the high street chemist.

If the idea of going into a sex shop demanding super-lube – 'A crate of your finest, bumming-quality lubricant, my good man, and be quick about it!' – is making you uncomfortable, there's no need: everything is available online. For All That Sort Of Thing, I recommend Sh![6] (and it's worth noting that their bricks-and-mortar shops are women-friendly, women-centred and staffed only by friendly, non-judgemental women).

More prosaically, soap is very drying: you may want to use a soap-free product instead. Wear 100 per cent cotton knickers, needless to say, not gross synthetic ones – cotton lets air in, while synthetics suffocate the PARTS, which at this stage is really a Pelion-upon-Ossa kind of situation.

If the pain or dryness problem is worse than this, then for heaven's sake see your doctor: **there is no need to have painful sex**. Better to be mildly embarrassed than to suffer the Death Of Shagging: this problem can be fixed. And anyway, it's not really that embarrassing at all, it happens to millions of women every year. If you go to the doctor's – well, I'm right there with you. We all are, in a metaphorical sisterly pod. Don't forget this. We are in the same boat. What will happen here is that you may be offered HRT, Hormone

[6] sh-womenstore.com

Replacement Therapy, which I'll get to in a bit, or an oestrogen cream to be applied topically (i.e. to the vagina). You may also be offered oestrogen pessaries, tablets, or an oestrogen-releasing ring that you insert and leave in place for around three months.

If you're perimenopausal, people speak with bated breath of the wonders of the Mirena coil supplemented with topical oestrogen (you can't have stand-alone oestrogen if you have a womb, only if you've had a hysterectomy). This combination of treatments minimizes the two main perimenopausal symptoms: the Mirena coil secretes a low-dose progestogen that controls heavy bleeding, while the topical oestrogen is good for the vaginal tissues.

What about Loss of Libido?

I must just repeat: an awful lot of women have the opposite 'problem'. Do not assume that loss of libido is what will happen to you.

Now: low libido, where it occurs, seems to be closely linked to the anxieties above: obviously, if having sex is painful, then you're hardly going to be bending over the kitchen table going 'Yoo-hoo' at every opportunity. It's also linked to feeling troubled and/or depressed and/or demented around the whole subject of the menopause. Your mood swings may be wild and may leave you feeling powerless; your night sweats and insomnia may come with nameless horrors attached. Loss of libido may also be linked to feeling unattractive and withered (see the whole of the rest of this book for ways of combatting that last one).

In the USA, you would be offered testosterone, which studies show helps with libido, arousal, sexual desire and easiness reaching orgasm. The snag is that the possible side effects are really not great: deepening of the voice and increase in facial hair. Testosterone, solo, used to be offered in the UK, either as a patch or as an implant, but the patch has been withdrawn and the implant is currently only available where clinics (usually private) are able to source the testosterone from outside the UK. On the NHS, at the time of writing, testosterone is only offered in conjunction with oestrogen.

For anxiety and depression, also see your doctor. Whether the Gobi Desert is going on in your pants or whether you're 'just' clinically depressed, help exists and is available to you. It is crazy-crazy, not just menopause-crazy, not to ask for it. Speaking of depression, there is a fairly persuasive school of thought that believes that depression at this age may be linked to loss of oestrogen; you may wish to discuss this with your doctor.

IF IT'S ALL DOWN TO HORMONES, CAN'T I JUST TAKE SOME?

This is the million-dollar question. Yes, you can. But taking one-size-fits-all hormones in the form of HRT – which replaces the hormones you are losing naturally with synthetic ones – is not a risk-free thing to do. (Having said that, I don't think HRT deserves its bad rep.) Plus, as we have seen at length, this whole business is the *opposite* of one-size-fits-all: each woman's experience is different. Here are some facts:

* HRT is categorically not a good idea if you have had **breast cancer, ovarian cancer or endometrial cancer**, and should be taken with caution if you have a family history of one of these.

* It's not for you if you have a history of **heart disease or stroke**, a history of **blood clots**, or **untreated high blood pressure**.

* According to the NHS,[7] the **side effects of taking synthetic oestrogen** include: fluid retention and bloating, sore and/or swollen breasts, nausea, leg cramps, headaches and indigestion.

* The **side effects of taking progesterone** include: fluid retention, headaches and breast

[7] There are many alleged other risks enumerated by alternative health practitioners. On the other hand, even aspirin comes with a list of fairly dramatic potential side effects.

tenderness (again), as well as depression, mood swings, backache and acne.

Will HRT Give Me Breast Cancer?

Possibly, yes, but keep reading. Cancer Research UK summarizes it thus (as of summer 2014):

1. Research shows that **taking HRT increases the risk of breast cancer**.

2. **Combined HRT** (oestrogen + progesterone) **increases the risk** more than oestrogen-only HRT.

3. **Women taking combined HRT have double the risk of breast cancer** compared to women who take no HRT; and the longer you take HRT, the more your risk increases.

4. However, **your risk goes back to normal within five years of stopping HRT**. So this is not a decision to be taken lightly, to say the least. Twenty years ago, HRT was the magic bullet. These days, well, you should decide for yourself – in conjunction with your doctor.

Here is an important thing to bear in mind, though. 'Doubling the risk' of breast cancer sounds like a no-brainer – nobody in their right mind would want that. But put another way, the statistics show that for every 1,000 women between the ages of fifty and sixty-five, 32 will develop breast cancer, rising to 56 in those taking HRT. That's still quite a big risk, but it's not as bad as it first sounds. The fact is, if you can't have sex, feel demented and are drenched in sweat fifteen times a day – plus the rest – then 'doubling the risk' might seem like an acceptable deal. Certainly the GPs I spoke to for this section of the book unanimously felt that the anti-HRT stuff had 'gone too far the other way. There are issues, yes, and it's important to make an informed decision. The fact remains: HRT can be transformative for some women.'

Here's another HRT scenario. Say you have a teensy, grain-of-rice-sized tumour in your breast. There it sits, too small to be detected by you or anybody else, quietly firing off and doing its hideous, decimating thing. Eventually – four or five or six or seven years later – it has grown big enough for you to feel it with your finger. You go to the doctor. To be brutal, it's too late: you've unknowingly had breast cancer for years. And so you die. Scenario B: you're on HRT. It is stimulating your breast tissue. The weensy lump is made bigger very – alarmingly – quickly. But you are much more medicalized than the above woman, and because you have an ongoing HRT-based relationship with your doctor, you get early diagnosis. The lump is spotted early; out it comes: you live.

This isn't to say that HRT is a panacea for the ills of middle-aged women. But nor is it necessarily the game of Russian roulette it's been depicted as in recent years. For what it's worth, I probably still wouldn't take it myself. Probably.

Interesting HRT fact: at one time there was a manufacturer that used not the urine of pregnant mares (Premarin is called Pre-mar-in for that reason: PREgnant MARe's urINe) but instead used the urine of an order of middle-aged nuns in Italy. Even better, this came about following an encounter between Dr Bruno Lunenfeld – who was the first person to study and assess the combination of testosterone and oestrogen in the menopause, in 1954 – and the nephew of Pope Pius XII.

What about the Amazing-Looking Older Celebs?

How do they look so good? You may be thinking, 'I bet *they* don't put themselves at risk of breast cancer.' There exist things called bio-identical hormones. This means that, unlike the synthetic hormones of normal HRT, these hormones (synthesized from yam and soy) are biologically identical to human hormones – exact duplications of the hormones produced by the female reproductive system. Their molecular structure is the same as that of the hormones your body produces: therefore, you whack 'em in and the body 'recognizes' them, and therefore – the theory goes – they are less likely to cause adverse reactions like cancer. On top of that, bio-identicals are tailored to the individual – created to fit the unique need of each patient, unlike one-size-fits-all ordinary HRT.

Sounds good, doesn't it? But bear in mind:

1. This is a **highly controversial** area. 'Natural' is not the same as 'safe'. One health professional told me: 'It's a middle-class racket – the equivalent of buying kale at Waitrose and pretending it's better than greens from the garden.' He did not think bio-identicals were less safe than normal HRT, though.

2. There are **specialists offering bio-identicals in the UK**. One is the Marion Gluck Clinic; another is the highly respected active birth pioneer Dr Yehudi Gordon. Both have comprehensive, information-heavy websites.[8]

3. They are, cumulatively, **monumentally expensive**.

4. This is arguable **slippery territory**: some people also swear by taking human growth hormone.

Not being a medical professional, I can give you this information but not pass further comment on it; if you have questions, always speak to your GP.

[8] mariongluckclinic.com and dryehudigordon.com

ARE THERE NON-LOONY NATURAL REMEDIES/SUPPLEMENTS THAT MIGHT HELP?

Anecdotally, yes. Evening primrose oil, black cohosh, pine bark, St John's wort are the ones that crop up most often as being effective – but the anecdotal evidence is rarely backed up by medical evidence. That doesn't mean they're no good, but it does still mean that 'natural' doesn't automatically equal 'safe'. *Always* speak to your doctor.

For a sane, fact-based, no-crazy-promises take on 'alternative' remedies I recommend Victoria Health. It's also one of my favourite websites for below-the-radar beauty products, and sends out excellent email newsletters.[9]

WHAT ABOUT THE PSYCHOLOGICAL EFFECTS OF MENOPAUSE?

Well, quite. Never underestimate the preconditioning of emotional responses. In other words, if you fully expect something to be an utter nightmare, it probably will be. If your experience of observing menopausal women is of observing ongoing drama, ditto. Also, some women do appear to temporarily lose their marbles around the menopause. And while there may be physiological

[9] victoriahealth.com

reasons for this, there are certainly contributing mental factors, too. The menopause is categorical, physical proof that a part of your life is over. You may have known, for instance, that you were increasingly unlikely to have children, but that doesn't mean it isn't a shock to know, for certain, that it is now never going to happen (it is also a shock for women who do have children. The idea of being fertile and then suddenly not is unpleasant and startling, even if it's hardly a surprise).

This period – the official entry into the final third of your life – is also apt to cause you to stand back from yourself and re-examine your life choices. If you're broadly pleased with them, then all well and good. If they cause you to think, 'I got it completely wrong; this is not how I wanted to end up,' that's not a good feeling. However, you have a third of your life left to remedy that, which should be a very cheering thought.

What Part Does Stress Play in All of This?

Stress is incredibly bad for you, which is why I keep exhorting you to live as well and as fully as you can. As we age, we need to find ways of either removing stress – something that is easier said than done – or of coping with it better.

It's unfortunate that we are taught to admire people whose entire professional lives are basically a manifestation of mega stress: long hours, very little sleep, running about, never staying still. There is, in fact, nothing admirable about any of these things: those people may end up running companies on three continents, but their quality of life is dreadful and they are very possibly making themselves ill.

Cortisol is the relevant hormone here. It is produced in the adrenal gland and allows the body to respond to all sorts of stress – from illness to an accident to three screaming toddlers freaking out at the same time. As we age, the systems that regulate stress hormones become weakened. The cortisol we produce doesn't work as well as it did. Also, having too much cortisol (as the result of living a stressful existence) impacts negatively on all sorts of things – from loss of muscle and gaining fat around the stomach to raised blood pressure, higher body mass and cholesterol, and a decrease in memory performance.

Do whatever you have to do to lessen your stress levels, even if it's something small and clichéd like going for a snooze, or having a massage (it doesn't have to cost money – a friend or partner can give you a massage, and you can reciprocate).

AFTERWORD

There's a whole third of life to go. That's not an ending – it's a thrilling new beginning. And as you approach the years ahead, you do so at the height of your powers. You know more than you've ever known. You are the wisest you've ever been. All your life experiences – your triumphs and your failures, your highs and your lows – have turned you into the fully rounded person you are today. You know yourself: if we could bottle the confidence and comfort that brings, we'd all be millionaires. Approach this new stage of life in the spirit of adventure, and an adventure is what you'll have. Embrace change: it is your friend and will lead you to exciting new places. Embrace what you have, too – your pleasures and pastimes, your family, your friends, your hobbies and your home, the people who love you and whom you love.

This is not a time to stress and fret unless you really, absolutely have to. I hate annoying American phrases like 'don't sweat the small stuff', but really – don't sweat the small stuff. Save your cortisol for the big, unavoidable things. Until they come along – and even when they do – the world is a beautiful and extraordinary place, and here you are, in it, in your Prime. You are a flower in full bloom.

One last thing: you really can't take it with you. Live as well as you can, and remember that tiny little things can bring as much pleasure as great big giant ones. Put on the radio, buy a bunch of flowers, open the window and look out. Being older doesn't mean that your whole future isn't ahead of you, shimmering. Use it wisely.

And above all, be happy.

APPENDIX 1

LASER EYE SURGERY

(This is a blog post I wrote on the day I had mine done. I regard the surgery as one of the best things I've ever done in my entire life. The second is stopping smoking: see page 187.)

I had my eyes lasered today. This isn't a newspaper article and I'm writing at speed, so let's do bullet points.

- I had (had!) myopia (short sight) and mild astigmatism; my prescription was −6 in one eye and −4 in the other.
- I've been wearing contact lenses since I was seventeen. I'm now forty-five. I didn't like the idea of keeping shoving bits of plastic in my eyes for all eternity.
- My eyes were permanently a tiny, tiny bit irritated − I was used to it and didn't feel discomfort, but the whites weren't as white as they might have been. Eh, vanity.
- More to the point, I hated being blind. I couldn't bear being in bed and not being able to see the time on the alarm clock, a couple

of feet away. On the very rare occasions that I wore my glasses, I felt ridiculously vulnerable, as you do if the only thing lying between you and blurry confusion/panic is a spindly pair of plastic specs.

- I used to wonder what I would do if something bad happened when I was lens-less – a fire, a burglar – and I had to grab my children and run and my glasses weren't immediately to hand. This made me feel anxious. So I decided – after years of being too scared, too grossed out, too worried, too incredulous – to investigate.

- Ask about laser surgery, and you'll get a wealth of opinion. The people who've had it done say: It's the best thing that ever happened to me. The sceptics say: You rarely meet an ophthalmologist who's had it done. Eye doctors all wear specs: QED.

- The sceptics have an excellent point. You don't meet many ophthalmologists who've had it done. Partly this is because most of us don't meet many ophthalmologists. Partly this is because privately many express doubt about the ubiquity of high street operations.

- This is because the procedure isn't a piece of cake but a serious, serious piece of surgery. It's your *eyes*, FFS. It's a major operation (even though it doesn't feel like it), and it's non-reversible. As one GP said to me – I did days of research – 'If you can't afford the absolute

best, don't have it done – simple as that.'
Actually, everyone said that.

- This isn't to say that all high street places are
  bad: some are great. But if you're going to go
  down that route:
  - Make sure your surgeon does some NHS
    work. If you're an ophthalmic surgeon and
    NHS-trained, you know your onions. The
    same isn't necessarily true of the private
    sector.   God bless the NHS.
  - Make sure your consultant is indeed a
    consultant and a member of the Royal
    College of Ophthalmologists.
  - Make sure the surgeon you see at the
    consultation will be the person carrying out
    the surgery – not a technician or a nurse or
    a random bod.
  - Make sure you ask how many times they've
    carried out the procedure.
  - Make sure they give you a proper, thorough
    examination. (Mine lasted, with breaks
    between bits, for just under three hours.)
- Armed with this information, which was vigor-
  ously repeated to me by every doctor I spoke
  to (four), I decided to forego the freebies I'd
  kindly been offered and pay my own money
  to go to Moorfields.
- I saw Mr (actually, Professor) David Gartry
  FRCS, the leading light in refractive laser
  surgery. He had the surgery himself ten years
  ago and was recommended to me by my GP

('I really don't want you to go to anyone else, apart from his colleague Julian Stevens'). Mr Gartry did my GP's eyes four years ago and has performed the procedure roughly 16,000 times to date.

What actually happens:

- You go for the consultation. It costs £175. It is long and comprehensive. The consultation establishes whether you are a suitable candidate.
- You then go for a chat with Mr Gartry, who answers all your questions, explains the risks and so on and so forth. He is very, very nice.
- NB: Most people (everyone, I mean, not just people with bad sight) will, from roughly their forties onwards, at some point need the kind of magnifying reading glasses you buy from the chemist. This is also the case after laser surgery. It is not currently the case for me, hooray, but I expect it will be at some point. It's just age – nothing you can do about it apart from being grateful for the fact you're not wearing contacts AND specs.
- You get anaesthetic drops at the consultation and you're very blurry for a couple of hours afterwards, so get someone to come and get you if that worries you (I walked home).
- Nothing they do hurts or freaks you out.
- I booked myself in there and then.

The surgery:

- You allow an hour for the procedure, although the actual time in the surgery room takes 15–20 minutes. The actual lasering is 30 seconds per eye.
- Everybody is incredibly nice and reassuring, even if you ask idiot questions.
- I'd taken half a Xanax, but you're offered magic pills if you need them (you don't. I wouldn't have bothered with the Xanax if I'd read this).
- The girl in before me came out just BEAMING and laughing with happiness, going 'Oh my God, oh my God, I can't believe it!' which was so cheering.
- It's a normal room with a chair that reclines.
- Nobody clamps your head! Though they used to. I'm intensely claustrophobic – not a figure of speech but properly, medically claustrophobic; I have to sedate myself to do certain things that involve enclosed spaces; I don't do lifts and so on. Fellow claustrophobes will understand that the idea of my head being clamped while my eyes were forcibly held open put me off – to the point of nightmares – for years.
- It is SO not like that.
- You just lie down. You're not clamped or held in any way. It's comfy.
- There are two separate machines – one to cut the corneal flap, one to fix the sight.

- They put in anaesthetic eyedrops, meaning that you feel nothing and that you're less likely to blink.
- One eye is covered and the other has this rubbery ring thing pinged in around your eye, making blinking even more unlikely. I didn't feel Mr Gartry put this in.
- The first machine flattens your eyeballs slightly to ready them, one at a time. Press your thumbs into your eye sockets – not very hard – and that's exactly the feeling. This lasts moments.
- Mr Gartry talked to me throughout, explaining what he was doing and counting me down – 'six seconds left', etc.
- The laser is then positioned. You stare at a red light for 30 seconds per eye. That's it.
- It can't fuck up. The laser cuts out if you blink or move your head.
- It's really, really interesting, from the consultation onwards. I was fascinated by the whole thing, especially laser number 2 today – looking at the lights is like looking at stars in space; it's beautiful.
- Yes, there is a smell. This also put me off for years. The smell is like hair burning – I've had worse with mishaps with straighteners, to be honest. I am extremely princessy and fastidious and I could barely summon up the interest to smell it.
- That's it.
- That's literally it.

- Maybe 15 minutes have elapsed since you entered the room.

What happens next:

- This depends on you and on your prescription. In my case, Mr Gartry had asked me to look at the clock before we started. I could barely locate it.
- When I hopped off the table and looked at it afterwards, I could tell the time – but as from behind a cloud of fog, or behind opaque glass. It was clear, but there was a mist.
- I was with a friend; we went for coffee and bacon butties. I wore sunglasses.
- We went home.
- You get given fake tear drops, antibiotic drops and anti-inflammatory drops. You put these in every hour, though not if you're sleeping (i.e. you don't wake yourself up to do it).
- I could already see better – the fog was lifting.
- I was seen at 10.30 a.m. By 2 p.m. I was back online and checking my emails.
- By 3 p.m. I was reading my book.
- It's now 9.40 p.m. and I can see better than I did with my lenses. This is quite trippy – be warned (I stared at a leaf for hours earlier).
- Mr Gartry says that this is nothing compared to how I will see in the morning.
- I have a follow-up appointment tomorrow.
- That's it. I'd blocked out two days, thinking

I'd lie in darkened rooms listening to the radio, but no. I'm bashing this out so I can get to the pub. You have to avoid smoky environments (myself, in my case) and you can't do massively physical stuff – martial arts, playing rugby – for a week or two. No eye make-up for the first week. You sleep in goggles – sexy – for the first week, so you don't accidentally rub your eyes and bugger up the corneal flap (sexy also). You wear sunglasses if you need to.

- I've had shit eyesight all my life. No more. I am seriously considering asking for flying lessons for Christmas to celebrate – I've always wanted to fly planes. Imagine wearing two hearing aids all your life and suddenly, after ZERO PAIN and 10–15 minutes, having perfect hearing. It's like that. It's a miracle. I would say I wish I'd had it done years ago – and I do – but the machinery was more imprecise. The stories you hear about haloes, driving at night and so on tend to be (though aren't exclusively) from people who had the procedure done over three years ago. The existing risks are all explained in the massive bumf you get sent when you book yourself in.
- This is my own, subjective experience with my particular prescription and this particular surgeon. Your mileage may vary. But in short: a miracle. Life is short and the world is beautiful – so much more beautiful than I ever knew. I do think the only drawback is the

320

amount of time I'm about to spend staring at things and marvelling. If you've ever wondered about it: do it.

- [My surgery cost £4,150 for both eyes; you can pay in instalments.]
- *Edited to add*: It's now just under 24 hours later and I've just had my check-up. 20/20 vision!

APPENDIX 2

COMFORT READS

Little Women by Louisa May Alcott
The Jackson Brodie books by Kate Atkinson
Persuasion by Jane Austen
Pride and Prejudice by Jane Austen
The L-Shaped Room by Lynne Reid Banks
Hens Dancing by Raffaella Barker
The Darling Buds of May books by H. E. Bates
  (these also work marvellously if you're feeling
  fat – bonus)
The Mapp and Lucia books by E. F. Benson
Circle of Friends by Maeve Binchy
Jane Eyre by Charlotte Brontë
Wuthering Heights by Emily Brontë
The Secret Garden by Frances Hodgson Burnett
The Miss Marple books by Agatha Christie
Riders and *Rivals* by Jilly Cooper (also the 'name'
  books – *Bella, Imogen,* etc.)
The Diary of a Provincial Lady by E. M. Delafield
Auntie Mame by Patrick Dennis
Mariana by Monica Dickens
The Dud Avocado by Elaine Dundy
Heartburn by Nora Ephron

Like Water for Chocolate by Laura Esquivel

Crooked Heart by Lissa Evans

Cold Comfort Farm by Stella Gibbons (also *Nightingale Wood* by the same author)

Travels with My Aunt by Graham Greene

The Diary of a Nobody by George and Weedon Grossmith

84 Charing Cross Road by Helene Hanff

Anything by Georgette Heyer – maybe start with *The Grand Sophy*

The Cazalet Chronicles by Elizabeth Jane Howard (bliss, plus there are tons of them)

Angry Housewives Eating Bon Bons by Lorna Landvik

Dusty Answer by Rosamond Lehmann

Invitation to the Waltz by Rosamond Lehmann

The Towers of Trebizond by Rose Macaulay

The Scotland Street books by Alexander McCall Smith

The Tales of the City series by Armistead Maupin

Frenchman's Creek by Daphne Du Maurier

Rebecca by Daphne Du Maurier

Gone with the Wind by Margaret Mitchell

The Pursuit of Love by Nancy Mitford (start there and read them all)

Excellent Women by Barbara Pym (and everything else she ever wrote)

The Lord Peter Wimsey books by Dorothy L. Sayers

Katherine by Anya Seaton

A Suitable Boy by Vikram Seth
The Guernsey Literary and Potato Peel Pie Society by
  Mary Ann Shaffer
I Capture the Castle by Dodie Smith
Miss Buncle's Book by D. E. Stevenson
Ballet Shoes by Noel Streatfeild
The Adrian Mole books by Sue Townsend
Miss Pettigrew Lives for a Day by Winifred Watson
Not That Sort of Girl by Mary Wesley
The Age of Innocence by Edith Wharton
Little House on the Prairie by Laura Ingalls Wilder
The Molesworth books by Geoffrey Willans and
  Ronald Searle
Forever Amber by Kathleen Windsor
Right Ho, Jeeves, Code of the Woosters and *Uncle Fred
in the Springtime* by P. G. Wodehouse (but any,
really)

APPENDIX 3

BRILLIANT COOKBOOKS

(An asterisk means you can learn to cook from scratch from any one of these books.)

These are my recommendations:

- *Perfect*★ and *Perfect Too*★ by Felicity Cloake
- All of Elizabeth David (perhaps more for reading than for recipes)
- *English Food* by Jane Grigson
- *Roast Chicken and Other Stories* and *The Good Cook* by Simon Hopkinson
- *How to Eat*★ and *Nigella Express* by Nigella Lawson
- New Voices in Food series, showcasing interesting young cooks (in particular *Small Adventures in Cooking* by James Ramsden and *Alice's Cookbook* by Alice Hart)
- *The Book of Middle Eastern Food* and *Arabesque: A Taste of Morocco, Turkey and Lebanon* by Claudia Roden
- *Eat: The Little Book of Fast Food,*★ *Real Food* and *Kitchen Diaries 1 & 2* by Nigel Slater (every home should have a copy of *Eat*, particularly)
- *One Good Dish* by David Tanis

All the recipes in these books are doable, but best when you have time, or at weekends, or in a pottery way:

- *Moro* and *Morito* by Samuel and Samantha Clark
- *River Café Cookbook* and *River Café Cookbook Easy* (books 1 & 2) by Rose Gray and Ruth Rogers
- *The Classic Italian Cookbook* by Marcella Hazan
- *Good Things to Eat* by Lucas Hollweg
- *Ottolenghi: The Cookbook, Plenty* and *Jerusalem* by Yotam Ottolenghi

These books are best for family cooking:

- *You're All Invited* by Margot Henderson
- *Home Cook** by Alastair Hendy
- *Cook Simple** by Diana Henry – my most used cookbook ever
- *Really Useful Cookbook** by David Herbert
- *Kitchen: Recipes from the Heart of the Home** by Nigella Lawson
- *Big Table, Busy Kitchen** by Allegra McEvedy
- *Jamie's Ministry of Food,* *Jamie's 30-Minute Meals* and *Jamie's Italian* by Jamie Oliver
- *Delia's Complete Cookery Course** and *Delia Smith's Christmas* by Delian Smith
- *River Cottage Every Day* and *River Cottage Veg Every Day!** by Hugh Fearnley-Whittingstall